On Target English

Comprehension and Writing Skills

Year 6

Hilary Frost
Sarah Lindsay
Heather Painter

Edinburgh Gate
Harlow, Essex

Contents

Black Beauty

Our master was a good, kind man. He gave us good food, good lodging, and kind words; he spoke as kindly to us as he did to his little children. We were all fond of him, and my mother loved him very much. When she saw him at the gate, she would neigh with joy, and trot up to him. He would pat and stroke her ... then he would give me a piece of bread, which was very good, and sometimes he brought a carrot for my mother. All the horses would come to him, but I think we were his favourites. My mother always took him to the town on a market day in a little gig.

There was a ploughboy, Dick, who sometimes came into our field to pluck blackberries from the hedge. When he had eaten all he wanted, he would have what he called fun with the colts, throwing stones and sticks at them to make them gallop. We did not much mind him, for we could gallop off; but sometimes a stone would hit and hurt us.

One day he was at this game, and did not know that the master was in the next field; but he was there, watching what was going on: over the hedge he jumped in a snap, and catching Dick by the arm, he gave him such a box on the ears as made him roar with the pain and surprise. As soon as we saw the master, we trotted up nearer to see what went on.

"Bad boy!" he said. "bad boy! to chase the colts. This is not the first time, nor the second, but it shall be the last – there – take your money and go home, I shall not want you on my farm again." So we never saw Dick any more. Old Daniel, the man who looked after the horses, was just as gentle as our master, so we were well off.

Anna Sewell

Life on the farm

Write a sentence to answer each of these questions:

1 What did Black Beauty's mother do when she saw the master?

2 What did the master bring for Black Beauty?

3 Where did Black Beauty's mother take the master?

4 What job did Dick do on the farm?

5 Why did Dick go to the horse field where the horses were?

6 Why didn't the horses mind too much about Dick throwing stones?

7 What did the master do when he caught Dick throwing stones?

Comprehension

- To respond accurately to literal questions

Helpful words

neigh piece
plough blackberries
avoid gallop

Finding out

Write a sentence to answer each of these questions:

1 From whose point of view is the story told?

2 Find the words in the text that mean the same as:
carriage pick

3 What actions show us that the master was a kind man?

4 Why do you think Dick started throwing sticks and stones at the colts?

5 What do you think the author means by 'he jumped in a snap'?

6 Do you think the master's punishment of Dick was right? Give reasons for your opinion.

Tip

Look out for questions that need extended answers.

Writing

- To write a story with two different narrators

Dick's story

1 **a** Describe Dick.
Use this table to help you.

Name or title	
Job	
His actions	
Words to describe him	

Tip

Include descriptions of what he did and what he was thinking about.

b Now tell the story from Dick's point of view.
Start your story like this:

It was a warm day in early autumn when I finished ploughing the long meadow. I was hot and tired so…

The master's story

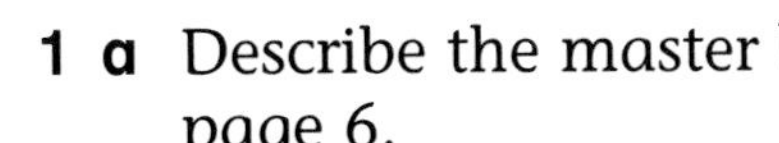

1 a Describe the master by using a table like the one on page 6.

b Now tell the story from the point of view of the master. Start your story like this:

I had been busy all morning repairing a hole in the hedge when I noticed in the next field …

Reread each part of the story you have written to edit and improve your work.

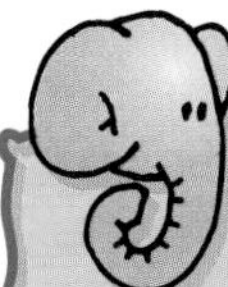

Remember

When editing your work you should check for:

- spelling errors
- punctuation
- best use of vocabulary.

Famous Victorians

Isambard Kingdom Brunel

1806–1859

We went down the shaft on the south bank, and got, with young Brunel, into a punt, which he was to steer into the tunnel ... Brunel, swinging carelessly from right to left, fell overboard, and out went the candles with which he was lighting up the place ... by the glimmering light from the entrance, we found young Brunel, who swam like a fish, coming up ... and soon got him on board.

This describes Isambard Kingdom Brunel at the age of twenty-one taking a party of visitors down into a tunnel flooded by river water. It clearly shows his fearless character. Brunel was managing the construction of his father's tunnel under the Thames. This tunnel took eighteen years to complete, mainly because the walls kept collapsing, letting in the river water.

Brunel entered a competition to design a bridge across the River Avon at Bristol. His winning entry was eventually to become the great Clifton Suspension Bridge.

Brunel then turned his mind to railways and won the job of surveying the land for the new railway to run between London and Bristol. The work had to be done on horseback and he was often riding for twenty hours a day. He was quite short but his personality and huge energy earned him the nickname of "Little Giant". There was a lot of opposition to the railway. The Duke of Wellington voiced the fears of many rich people when he expressed his worries that the railway "would encourage the lower classes to move about".

Within a few years Brunel had built the biggest ship in the world, the *Great Western*, designed to cross the Atlantic Ocean. On its first voyage it caught fire, however, and Brunel fell down a deep hatch as he rushed to put out the blaze. He recovered and went on to build the first steamship to be made of iron instead of wood – the *Great Britain*. But it was his attempt to build a ship big enough to carry its own coal between Britain and Australia that was his hardest task. The *Great Eastern*, as it was called, had many problems and Brunel worried so much about it that he became ill. He was lying in bed, gravely ill, when the *Great Eastern* finally set off on its first voyage. It exploded before it reached the open sea. Shortly after hearing this sad news, Brunel died. But his great ship survived.

"By his death the greatest of England's engineers was lost, the man with the greatest originality of thought and power of execution, bold in his plans but right."

So said his friend, the engineer Daniel Gooch. Yet this was not everyone's opinion at that time. An article written for *The Field* just months before, said:

If great engineering consists in effecting huge monuments of folly [madness] at enormous cost to shareholders, then is Mr Brunel surely the greatest of engineers...

Adapted from History Makers: Victorians *by Clare Chandler*

1806 Isambard Kingdom Brunel is born.

1815 George Stephenson builds the first efficient steam locomotive.

1825 Work begins on the Thames tunnel.

1826 Brunel becomes an engineer in charge of the tunnel works.

1829 George Stephenson builds *The Rocket*, a famous locomotive.

1831 Brunel's design is chosen for the Clifton Bridge.

1833 Starts survey for the Great Western Railway.

1836 Marriage to Mary Horsley. Construction of the Clifton Bridge begins.

1838 *Great Western* steamship is launched and crosses the Atlantic in fifteen days.

1841 Great Western Railway opens.

1843 Thames Tunnel opens. *Great Britain* steamship is launched.

1844 Bristol and Exeter Railway opens.

1854 Work on the *Great Eastern* begins.

1855 Designs a ready-made hospital for use in the Crimean War.

1859 *Great Eastern's* first voyage. Brunel dies. Royal Albert Bridge at Saltash is completed.

1860 *Great Eastern* sails to New York.

Fact or opinion

Write *fact* or *opinion* for each of these sentences:

1 Brunel's response to his accident in the tunnel shows his fearless character.
2 He won a competition to design a bridge.
3 It was unsuitable for the lower classes to move about the country on trains.
4 The *Great Western* caught fire on its first voyage.
5 Brunel died because he heard the sad news about the explosion on the *Great Eastern*.
6 Brunel was the greatest of England's engineers in Victorian times.
7 Brunel's work was original in design.

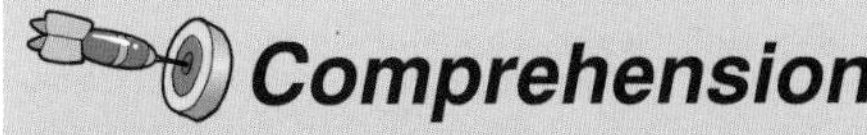

Comprehension

- To distinguish between fact and opinion

Clifton Bridge | The *Great Western*

Brunel's achievements

Some questions will require more than one sentence to answer.

1 Why do you think candles were used to light the tunnel under the Thames?
2 Why were some people against the building of railways? Can you think of more reasons than the one in the passage?
3 Explain why Brunel was nicknamed 'Little Giant'.
4 Look carefully at the two ways information about Brunel has been presented. Decide which would be more useful if you had to write an introduction to a television programme about him, and give the reasons for your choice.
5 Opinions about Brunel's achievements varied. Explain which you agree with, and say why.

Helpful words

some people thought that
invented
point of view
character
engages the interest
disagree/agree
with the opinion
monuments
my opinion is

Writing

- To consider ways of presenting biographical material

Writing a curriculum vitae

A curriculum vitae (CV for short) is a way of presenting information about a person for others to use, e.g. when you are applying for a job. It is a brief summary of a person's life, concentrating on their interests and achievements.

Elizabeth Fry

Soup Kitchen

Newgate Prison

Elizabeth Fry

Elizabeth Gurney, born into a rich family on 21 May 1780, soon wanted to help people who were less fortunate than herself. Growing up in a large, happy, wealthy family in Norfolk, she was soon aware of the difference between her life and the lives of the local villagers.

As soon as she was married, and became Elizabeth Fry, she started a school for poor children in her village and a soup kitchen to ensure that no one in the village, however poor, would ever go hungry. She vaccinated as many people as she could to ensure the area was kept free from smallpox, a deadly disease in Victorian Britain.

Apart from her natural kindness, Elizabeth Fry was inspired by her strong religious beliefs as a Quaker. Although the rest of her family were more relaxed, and wore fashionable clothes, and enjoyed music and dancing, Elizabeth became very strict, wearing simple, plain clothes and a plain white cap.

In 1813, a bitterly cold winter, Elizabeth Fry had heard about the terrible conditions of women prisoners in Newgate Prison in London. She collected warm clothes and blankets from some of her rich friends and took them to the prison. But she was so shocked by the misery she saw that she decided to make it her life's work to change conditions in prisons, not just for women, and not just in Britain, but across Europe for men and women alike.

Mrs Fry believed that if prisoners had useful things to do there would be an end to drunkenness and fighting. She wanted to help the prisoners at Newgate become better people, so she organised a school, where the women were taught to read, write and sew. They could then make things which could be sold to make a little money.

The change she brought the Newgate Prison was extraordinary, and many people were impressed, including her brother-in-law who was an MP. He persuaded Parliament to change the law about prisons.

In 1819, another severe winter, Elizabeth Fry and some helpers opened a soup kitchen and warehouse for the homeless in London. She did all this work as well as bringing up eleven children of her own! She eventually died in 1845.

Use the information about Elizabeth Fry to write a curriculum vitae for her.

Use this form to help you:

Married name ....

Maiden name ....

Date of birth ....

Main achievements ....

....

....

Interests/hobbies ....

....

....

....

Remember

The prefix ***auto*** means **self**.

Tip

To help you, look at the way paragraphs have been used in the text on page 10.

Writing an autobiography

Imagine you are Elizabeth Fry. Rewrite her biographical account in the words she might have used.

Remember that you are writing about yourself as Elizabeth Fry, so this is an autobiography.

Start your autobiography like this:

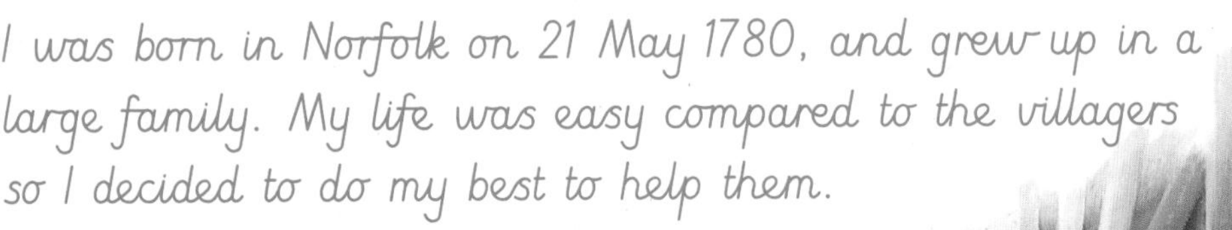

I was born in Norfolk on 21 May 1780, and grew up in a large family. My life was easy compared to the villagers so I decided to do my best to help them.

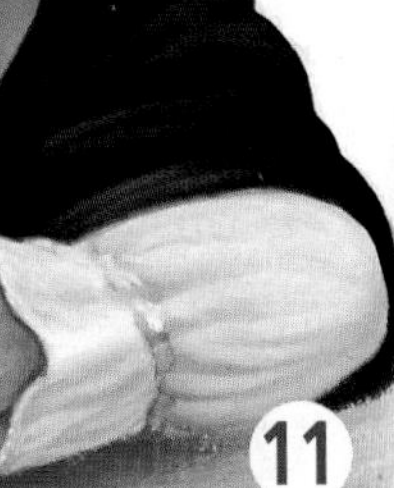

The Sea

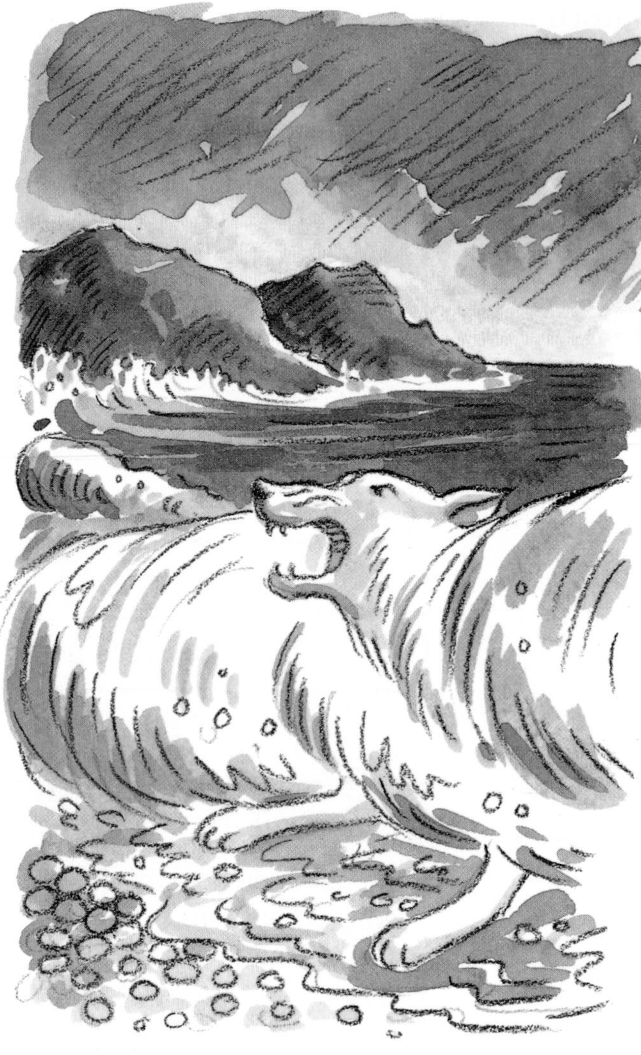

The Sea

The sea is a hungry dog,
Giant and grey.
He rolls on the beach all day.
With his clashing teeth and shaggy jaws
Hour upon hour he gnaws
The rumbling, tumbling stones,
And "Bones, bones, bones, bones!"
The giant sea dog moans,
Licking his greasy paws.

And when the night wind roars
And the moon rocks in the stormy cloud,
He bounds to his feet and snuffs and sniffs,
Shaking his wet sides over the cliffs,
And howls and hollos long and loud.

But on quiet days in May or June,
When even the grasses on the dune
Play no more their reedy tune,
With his head between his paws
He lies on the sandy shores,
So quiet, so quiet, he scarcely snores.

James Reeves

Sea Fever

I must go down to the seas again, to the lonely sea and the sky,
And all I ask is a tall ship and a star to steer her by;
And the wheel's kick and the wind's song and the white sail's shaking,
And a grey mist on the sea's face, and a grey dawn breaking.

...

I must go down to the seas again, to the vagrant gypsy life,
To the gull's way and the whale's way, where the wind's like a whetted knife;
And all I ask is a merry yarn from a laughing fellow-rover,
And quiet sleep and a sweet dream when the long trick's over.

John Masefield

Glossary
whetted *sharpened*

Are they similar?

Fill in the missing sections of this table. Some have been started but not completed.

Comprehension

- To examine and compare two poems

Poem title	The Sea	Sea Fever
Poet		
Number of verses		
Number of lines in each verse		
Words that rhyme at the end of lines	grey, day;	
The poet's point of view		The poet is away from the sea and longing to be back there again.
What the sea is like in the poem	rough,	lonely,
Favourite line in each poem		

Helpful words

rough motion
incessant splashing
calm tranquil
stormy imagine
longing memories
cutting

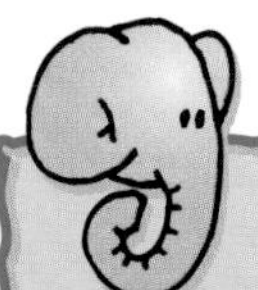

Remember

If something is described as if it is something else, it is called a **metaphor**.

Moods of the sea

1 These lines are taken from the poem *The Sea*.
Explain what you think the poet might mean by these lines.

a he gnaws
The rumbling, tumbling stones

b Shaking his wet sides over the cliffs

c With his head between his paws
He lies on the sandy shores

2 Read the first verse of the *The Sea* again. Write in your own words what you think the sea looks like.

3 In the poem *Sea Fever* what kind of boat is referred to?

4 From the poem *Sea Fever* write three things that the poet really misses about the sea.

5 What does the poet mean by the phrase *'the wind's like a whetted knife'*?

6 Which of these two poems was probably written first? Give a reason for your answer.

7 Which poem do you prefer? Give your reasons.

Sorting ideas

The wind, in its different moods, can be like different animals. Which animal do you think of, and what is it doing, when the wind is:

howling between the buildings
whispering through the trees
making a cold draught in the house
flickering flames in a fire
blowing umbrellas inside out
carrying a dandelion seed along
breaking branches off a tree

Writing a poem

Use some of the ideas you have written down to help you write a poem about the wind.

Before you start, decide whether or not you want the poem to rhyme.

Start your poem like this:

When the wind is howling between the buildings

It is a wolf, desperately searching for its lost cubs.

When the wind is …

When you have edited your poem copy it out neatly and illustrate it.

Writing

- To write your own poem, experimenting with ideas

Helpful words

angrily gently
quietly silently
raging stealthily
roaring creeping
devouring playing
nudging pushing

Tip

In your poem, the wind can be like different animals in its different moods.

Remember

Edit your work by taking out words that are not needed and improve it by adding more imaginative words and phrases.

Tom's Midnight Garden

When the clock struck thirteen, Tom found his way into a beautiful garden. It was all there for him to explore but he was not free to roam everywhere.

Tom glared at the door that once more was his barrier. Once more, without hope, he raised his hand to the latch and pressed it. As usual, he could not move it: his fingers seemed to have no substance. Then, in anger, he pressed with all imaginable might: he knitted his brows, and brought all his will to bear upon the latch, until he felt that something had to happen. It did: his fingers began to go through the latch, as though the latch, and not his fingers, now, were without substance. His fingers went through the ironwork of the latch altogether, and his hand fell back into place by his side.

Tom stared down at the ever-memorable right hand. He felt it tenderly with his left, to see if it were bruised or broken: it was quite unhurt – quite as before. Then he looked at the latch: it looked as real as any latch he had ever seen anywhere.

Then the idea came to Tom that the door might be no more solid than the latch, if he really tried it.

Deliberately he set his side against the door, shoulder, hip and heel, and pressed. At first, nothing gave, either of himself or the door. Yet he continued the pressure, with still greater force and greater determination; and gradually he became aware of a strange sensation, that at first he thought was a numbness all down his side – but no, it was not that.

"I'm going through," Tom gasped, and was seized with alarm and delight.

On the other side of the wall, the gardener had emptied his barrow-load of weeds and was sitting on the handle of his barrow, in front of a potting-shed, eating his midday dinner. If he had been able to see Tom at all he would have seen a most curious sight: a very thin slice of boy, from shoulder to foot, coming through a perfectly solid wooden door. At first the body came through evenly from top to bottom; then, the upper part seemed to stop, and the bottom part came through in its entirety, legs first. Then one arm came through, then another. Finally, everything was through except the head ...

With a convulsive effort, eyes closed, lips sealed, Tom dragged his head through the door, and stood, dizzy, dazed, but whole, on the far side of it.

Philippa Pearce

Glossary

substance	*solid presence*
convulsive	*sudden and violent*

Comprehension

- To provide accurate information about the passage

Helpful words

worried ghost
substance angry
remarkable unable
annoyed unusual
frustrated excited

Beyond the wall

Choose the correct answer for each question:

1 What was Tom trying to get through?
a garden gate, a garden door, a garden fence

2 What began to go through the latch and gave Tom the idea he might be able to get through the door?
his head, his fingers, his elbow

3 How did Tom's hand feel after it had been through the latch?
bruised, unhurt, broken

4 Where was the gardener sitting?
in the potting shed, on his wheelbarrow, on top of the wall

5 What did Tom have to be to get through the door?
fearful, anxious, determined

6 How did Tom feel when he had passed through the door?
dizzy, nervous, bored

Going through

Write a sentence to answer each of these questions:

1 From whose point of view does the author tell the story?

2 How do you think Tom felt when he first stood in front of the door?

3 Why did Tom raise his hand to the latch 'without hope'?

4 Why does the author describe Tom's hand as 'ever-memorable'?

5 Why do you think Tom 'was seized with alarm and delight' as he began to go through the door?

6 Why do you think Tom was able to pass through the door?

7 Copy out the sentence that you like best. Give reasons for your choice.

Keep it brief

Writing

- To summarise a passage

Tom glared at the door that once more was his barrier. Once more, without hope, he raised his hand to the latch and pressed it. As usual, he could not move it: his fingers seemed to have no substance. Then, in anger, he pressed with all imaginable might: he knitted his brows, and brought all his will to bear upon the latch, until he felt that something had to happen. It did: his fingers began to go through the latch, as though the latch, and not his fingers, now, were without substance. His fingers went through the ironwork of the latch altogether, and his hand fell back into place by his side. (112 words)

When you summarise a passage include the main points:

Tom glared at the door and then raised his hand to press the latch. He could not move it but then he pressed so hard that in his mind something had to happen. It did; his fingers passed right through the latch. (42 words)

Summarise each of these sentences. You can take out phrases that are not needed and add words of your own.

1 *He felt it tenderly with his left, to see if it were bruised or broken: it was quite unhurt — quite as before.*
2 *At first the body came through evenly from top to bottom; then, the upper part seemed to stop, and the bottom part came through in its entirety, legs first. Then one arm came through, then another. Finally, everything was through except the head ...*
3 *With a convulsive effort, eyes closed, lips sealed, Tom dragged his head through the door, and stood, dizzy, dazed, but whole, on the far side of it.*

Writing a summary

Summarise this passage in not more than 50 words.
Write it in rough first so that you can make sure it is the correct length.
Then write it neatly in your book.

On the other side of the wall, the gardener had emptied his barrow-load of weeds and was sitting on the handle of his barrow, in front of a potting-shed, eating his midday dinner. If he had been able to see Tom at all he would have seen a most curious sight: a very thin slice of boy, from shoulder to foot, coming through a perfectly solid wooden door. At first the body came through evenly from top to bottom; then, the upper part seemed to stop, and the bottom part came through in its entirety, legs first. Then one arm came through, then another. Finally, everything was through except the head ... (111 words)

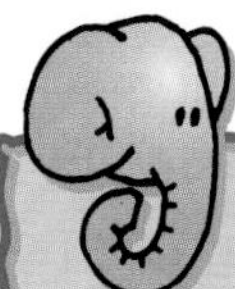

Remember

Check that the meaning is clear and that the main points are included.

Two Fables

The Fig Tree

Once upon a time there was a fig tree that had no fruit. Everyone passed by without looking at it.

In spring it put forth its leaves, but in summer, when the other trees were laden with fruit, nothing at all appeared on its branches.

"I would so love to have men praise me," sighed the fig tree. "All I want is to bear fruit like the other trees."

It tried and tried again, until at last, one summer, it too was laden with fruit. The sun caused the figs to grow and swell and made them sweet and fragrant.

People noticed this. Never before had they seen a fig tree so laden with fruit. And at once it was a race to see who could pick the most. They clambered up the trunk. They bent the highest branches with sticks, and some they broke off with their weight. Everyone tried to steal the delicious figs, and very soon the poor fig tree was all bent and broken.

So: those who cry out for attention may find, to their sorrow, that they receive more than they want.

Leonardo da Vinci

The Flea and the Sheep

A flea, who lived in the smooth hair of a dog, one day noticed the pleasant smell of wool.

"What is going on?"

He gave a little jump and saw that his dog had gone to sleep leaning against the fleece of a sheep.

"That fleece is exactly what I need," said the flea. "It is thicker and softer, and above all safer. There is no risk of meeting the dog's claws and teeth which go in search of me every now and then. And the sheep's wool will certainly feel more pleasant."

So without thinking too much about it, the flea moved house, leaping from the dog's coat to the sheep's fleece. But the wool was thick, so thick and dense that it was not easy to penetrate to the skin.

He tried and tried, patiently separating one strand from another, and laboriously making a way through. At last he reached the roots of the hair. But they were so close together that they practically touched. The flea had not even a tiny hole through which to attack the skin.

Tired, bathed in sweat and bitterly disappointed, the flea resigned himself to going back to the dog. But the dog had gone away.

Poor flea! He wept for days and days with regret for his mistake.

Leonardo da Vinci

Sorting sentences

Write these sentences in the correct order so that they tell the stories:

The Fig Tree

- *No one took any notice of it because it had no fruit.*
- *The branches became damaged when people climbed the tree to get the fruit.*
- *One sunny summer the fig tree was laden with plump, sweet figs.*
- *There was once a fig tree that bore no fruit.*
- *Everyone admired the fruit and tried to pick them.*

The Flea and the Sheep

- *He decided to return to the dog but the dog had gone away.*
- *He thought he would be much safer living on the sheep so he moved house.*
- *The flea noticed the dog had gone to sleep beside a sheep.*
- *There was a flea that lived in the smooth hair of a dog.*
- *The sheep's fleece was so thick that the flea could not penetrate it.*

- To compare two fables

Tip

A fable is a story that gives a moral lesson.

Comparing stories

Fill in this table with information from the stories. Leave enough space in the table to write notes or sentences.

	The Fig Tree	The Flea and the Sheep
Author		
Type of story		
Main character		
What the main character wanted		
What happened when they achieved what they wanted		
Moral of the story		

Helpful words

preferred admired noticed disappointed damaged regret attention mistake error

Morals from fables

Writing

- To write your own fable

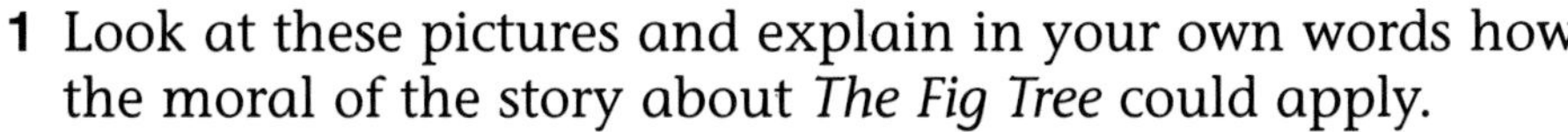

1 Look at these pictures and explain in your own words how the moral of the story about *The Fig Tree* could apply.

2 Write about an incident, when you chose to do something that you thought would be fun or would be interesting but afterwards you regretted it.

Helpful words

enjoyable criticism recognised private intrusion unnecessary attention

Writing a fable

Use a table like the one on the previous page to plan your own fable.

You could choose one of these issues to use as the moral to your story.

- Be cautious before you do something or you may get into trouble.
- Don't be greedy or disaster might strike.
- If you don't keep a friend's secret you can end up losing their trust.
- Think twice before you speak.
- A sad end may come to a clever person who wastes their talents.

Write your fable in your book. Remember to give it a title.

Tip

Fables often have animals as their main characters.

Britain's Sharks Face Extinction

For centuries, the basking shark has made a summer pilgrimage to Britain. Now it is facing extinction – the victim of foreign fishermen who slaughter it for its enormous dorsal fin, a delicacy in the Far East where it can fetch up to £20,000 a tonne.

The shark is the equivalent of the African rhino but far more mysterious. Weighing up to five tonnes, the creatures can be seen hurtling two metres above the sea – performing majestic half somersaults.

But this magnificent sight is becoming more rare. The number of sightings decreased by 80 per cent in the past seven years. So little is known about the shark and so great is the concern for its fate, that the Wildlife Trust and the Worldwide Fund for Nature have set up a group, called Seaquest, to monitor numbers over the next three years.

The basking shark is particularly vulnerable to hunting because it reproduces infrequently and the young are slow to mature. "If you start killing them the numbers decrease catastrophically," said Colin Speedie, a marine naturalist and project director of Seaquest.

The sharks appear off the west coast of Britain during the summer on their way between Iceland and Portugal. Previous attempts to track them have failed because, it is thought, they hibernate in deep canyons on the seabed.

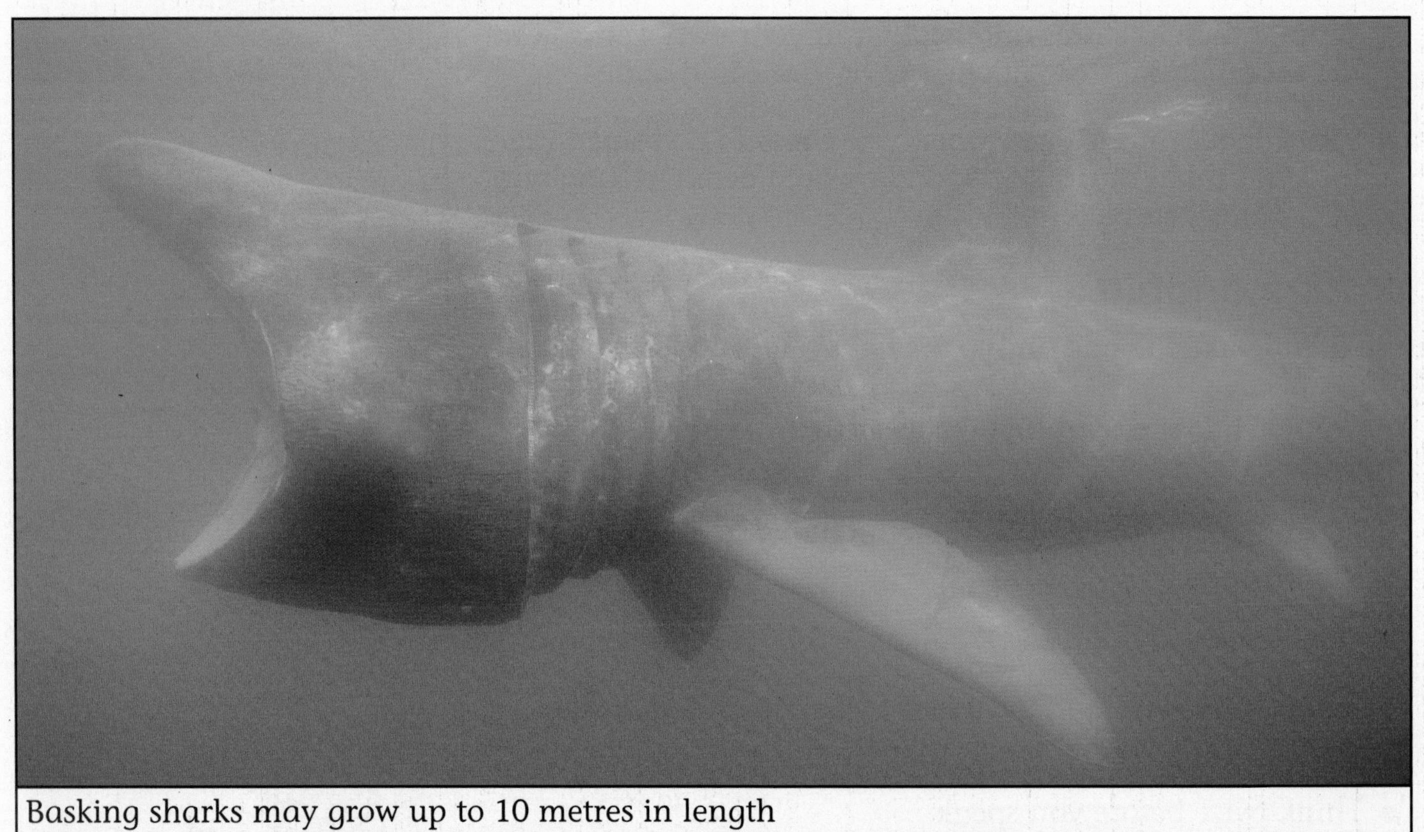

Basking sharks may grow up to 10 metres in length

The sharks were once caught to provide special oils for cosmetics and aircraft, but now they are in enormous demand for use in shark's fin soup, a Chinese delicacy. It is a quick, easy and financially rewarding business. A basking shark can be harpooned, stripped of its fins and the carcass dumped overboard within ten minutes. Environmentalists are pinning their hopes on securing an agreement at the Convention of the International Trade in Endangered Species, which would cut back the numbers killed.

MONSTERS THAT GATHER OFF BRITAIN'S HOLIDAY COASTS, BUT ARE A DANGER TO NO ONE!

- The basking shark is the second largest fish in the world (after the whale shark) and the largest in British waters.
- Maximum recorded length: 10 metres.
- Maximum weight: 5 tonnes.
- The young measure up to 2 metres at birth but are rarely seen until they reach more than 3 metres.
- Harmless to humans, they filter 9,000 litres of water an hour for plankton.
- Found off the western and south-western coast of Britain in summer; their winter waters are not known.
- Occasionally found alone, but usually in small groups, though shoals of 50 to 100 are known. A record shoal of 500 were sighted off Cornwall last year.

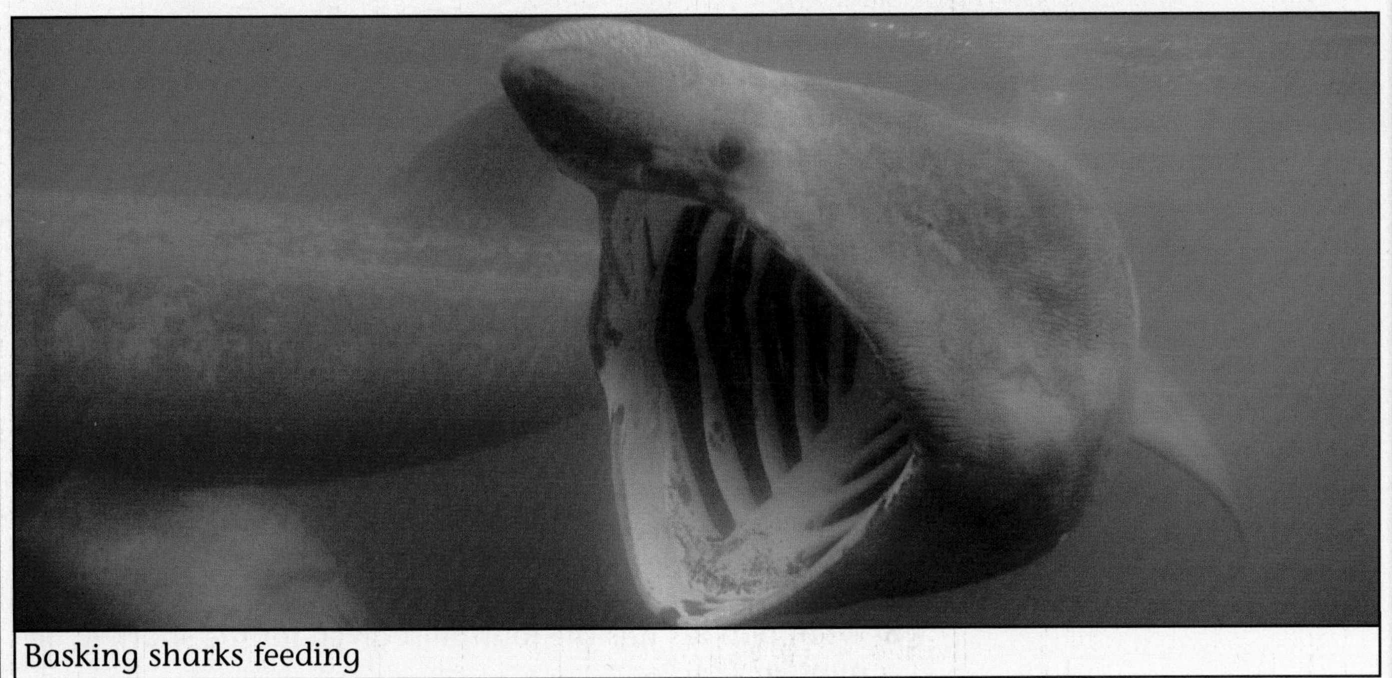

Basking sharks feeding

Adapted from an article by Mark Rowe in the Independent on Sunday

Comprehension

- To understand the features of a newspaper article

Tip

Use a dictionary to help you.

Words and their meanings

Match the words of similar meaning and provide five more to complete the list.

pilgrimage	________
slaughter	meeting
delicacy	________
equivalent	zoologist
monitor	________
vulnerable	defenceless
decrease	________
catastrophic	titbit
naturalist	________
convention	check

Helpful words

facts discussion
expectation reproduces
slaughtered matures
arguments expert
reinforces convincing

The job of the journalist

1 Why has the article on pages 24 and 25 got two distinctive parts?

2 Why do you think the journalist has made a point of saying 'Harmless to humans'?

3 Give three reasons why the basking shark is becoming an endangered species.

4 Write the words from the first paragraph that introduce the problem of the sharks to the reader.

5 What reasons has the journalist given for the shark to be hunted?

6 Do you think the journalist has provided a balanced view of the subject? Why?

7 Why do you think the journalist has quoted the words that Colin Speedie said?

Being a journalist

Imagine you are a journalist and have been asked to follow up these stories:

- A pig escapes from its pen and ends up in a school playground.
- There has been a storm which has caused a lot of damage.
- A boy has invented a game called Zoom but some people think it is dangerous.

Well, it did cause excitement among the children but our caretaker was magnificent and managed to corner the pig behind the bins.
There was this enormous bang and then part of the ceiling cracked, and the noise of slates could be heard smashing on the pavement.
They shouldn't be allowed. My toddler was holding my hand but it flew by her ear and she was terrified.

1 Write three questions you would like to ask each of these people. Record what you think their answers might be.

2 Think of a headline for each of these articles.

Writing the article

Choose **one** of the sets of questions and answers that you have written and enlarge it into a newspaper article.

- Invent names, times and places for your article.
- Decide what exactly happened.
- Decide which quotes you are going to use from your eyewitness accounts.
- Select a suitable headline.

Writing

- To write a lively, interesting article for a newspaper

Remember

When planning your questions, think what might interest your reader and present a balanced view of the subject.

Tip

Before you start, think about:

- the background information you need
- the order of events you need to write about
- the people you need to interview.

The Children of the New Forest

This story is set just after the English Civil War in the seventeenth century. The children, Edward, Humphrey, Alice and Edith, have been hidden from their father's enemies, in a cottage in the New Forest owned by Jacob Armitage. The troopers are approaching the cottage and the children are concealed upstairs in bed.

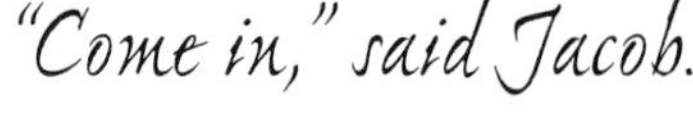

"Come in," said Jacob.

"Who are you, my friend?" said the leader of the troop, entering the door.

"A poor forester, sir," replied Jacob, "under great trouble."

"What trouble, my man?"

"I have the children all in bed with the smallpox."

"Nevertheless, we must search your cottage."

"You are welcome," replied Jacob, "only don't frighten the children if you can help it."

The man, who was now joined by others, commenced his search. They searched thoroughly, and then came back into the front room.

"It's no use remaining here," said one of the troopers. "Shall we be off? I'm tired and hungry with the ride."

"So am I; and there's something that smells well," said another. "What's this, my good man?" continued he, taking off the lid of the pot.

"My dinner for a week," replied Jacob. "I have no one to cook for me now, and can't light a fire everyday."

"Well, you appear to live well, if you have such a mess as that every day in the week. I should like to try a spoonful or two."

"And welcome, sir," replied Jacob, "I will cook some more for myself."

The troopers sat down to the table, and very soon the whole contents of the kettle had disappeared. Having satisfied themselves, they got up and rode away.

"Well," said Jacob, "they are very welcome to the dinner; I little thought to get off so cheap." As soon as they were out of sight Jacob called to Edward and the children to get up again, which they soon did.

"They're gone now," said Jacob, coming from the door.

"And our dinners are gone," said Humphrey, looking at the empty pot and dirty platters.

"Yes; but we can cook another."

"I hope it will be as good," observed Humphrey, "that other did smell so nice!"

"Quite as good, if not better; for we shall improve by practice, and we shall have a better appetite to eat it with," said Jacob.

And so they did as soon as it was cooked; but they were very hungry before they sat down.

Captain Frederick Marryat

Comprehension

- To understand the feelings and actions of characters in a story

The raid

Write only the statements that are true:

- Jacob was a poor forester.
- The children were in bed with smallpox.
- The troopers searched the cottage.
- Jacob was chopping vegetables for his stew.
- The troopers were hungry because they had been out all night.
- The troopers left their dirty dishes behind when they left.
- The troopers left the cottage on horseback.
- The children had a better appetite when they eventually got their meal.

Searching the cottage

1 Why did Jacob say that the children had smallpox?

2 What reason did Jacob give for having so much food?

3 Why did Jacob say that the troopers were welcome to eat the food?

4 How do you think the children felt when the troopers were searching the cottage?

5 What did Jacob mean when he said, "I little thought to get off so cheap"?

6 What reasons did Jacob give for the second meal being better than the first?

Helpful words

supply friendly
suspicion fearful
anxious trouble
ransacked hungry
practice

Writing a play script

1 It's no use remaining here. Shall we be off? I'm tired and hungry with the ride.
2 So am I; and there's something that smells well. What's this my good man?

Writing

- To turn part of a story into a play script

When turning this story into a play script it is necessary to indicate the following:

- the setting – where and when the action takes place
- the characters – who is speaking
- the stage directions – instructions to performers (how to speak and move)
- the dialogue – what the characters say

Copy the start of the play and continue it.

Scene 1: The Civil War has ended but danger is all around. Inside a simply furnished cottage, a pot is cooking over an open fire.

(Jacob is moving towards the door.)

JACOB Come in.

TROOP LEADER (entering through the door) Who are you, my friend?

Tip

List your characters before you start. You may have to indicate the different troopers by using numbers, e.g. Trooper One.

Out in the forest

Quick! We must hide.
I think we'll rest here and water the horses.

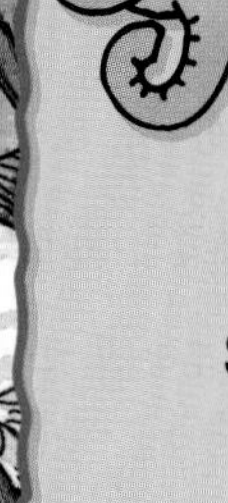

Remember

Setting
Characters
Stage directions
Dialogue

Look at the picture and imagine what might happen. Now write another scene for your play.

Prince Cinders

Prince Cinders was not much of a prince. He was small, spotty, scruffy and skinny. He had three big hairy brothers who were always teasing him about his looks. They spent their time going to the Palace Disco with their princess girlfriends. They made poor Cinders stay behind and clean up after them. When his work was done he would sit by the fire and wish he were big and hairy like his brothers.

One Saturday night, when he was washing the socks, a dirty fairy fell down the chimney.

"All your wishes shall be granted," cried the fairy.

"Ziz Ziz Boom, Tic Tac Ta,
This empty can shall be a car.
Biff Bang Bong, Bo Bo Bo,
To the disco you shall go.

That can't be right!" said the fairy.

"Toe of rat and eye of newt, your rags will turn into a suit!"

("Crumbs," thought the fairy, "I didn't mean a SWIM suit!") "Your greatest wish I'll grant you. You SHALL be big and hairy too."

Prince Cinders got big and hairy all right!

"Rats!" said the fairy. "Wrong again, but I'm sure it all wears off at midnight."

Prince Cinders did not know he was a big hairy monkey because that's the kind of spell it was. He thought he looked pretty good!

So off he went to the disco. The car was too small to drive but he made the best of it. But when he arrived at the Royal Rave up, he was too big to fit through the door! He decided to take the bus home. A pretty princess was waiting at the stop.

"When's the next bus?" he grunted.

Luckily midnight struck and Prince Cinders changed back into himself. The princess thought he had saved her by frightening away the big hairy monkey!

"Wait," she shouted, but Prince Cinders was too shy. He even lost his trousers in the rush!

The princess was none other than the beautiful Princess Lovelypenny. She put out a proclamation to find the owner of the trousers. Every prince from miles around tried to force the trousers on. But they wriggled about and refused to fit any of them. Of course Prince Cinders' brothers all fought to get into the trousers at once …

"Let him try," commanded the princess, pointing at Cinders.

"They won't fit that little squirt," sneered his brothers.

… But they did.

So Prince Cinders married Princess Lovelypenny and lived in luxury, happily ever after …

And Prince Cinders had a word with the fairy about his big hairy brothers … whom she turned into house fairies. And they flitted round the palace doing the housework for ever and ever.

Babette Cole

Comprehension

- To identify changes to a traditional story

Cinders – prince or poor girl?

The story of Prince Cinders is based on the traditional tale of Cinderella.

Compare what happens in the two stories by filling in the second column. Write both lists in your book.

Cinderella	Prince Cinders
1 Cinderella is a girl who has two older sisters.	1
2 Her sisters are ugly and make her do all the work around the house.	2
3 Cinderella wishes she had a beautiful dress and could go to the ball.	3
4 Her fairy godmother is pretty and her magic spells work properly.	4
5 The fairy godmother changes a pumpkin into a carriage.	5
6 Cinderella goes to the ball but has to leave at midnight.	6
7 In her haste to leave she loses a glass slipper.	7
8 The prince finds the girl who fits the slipper and marries her.	8

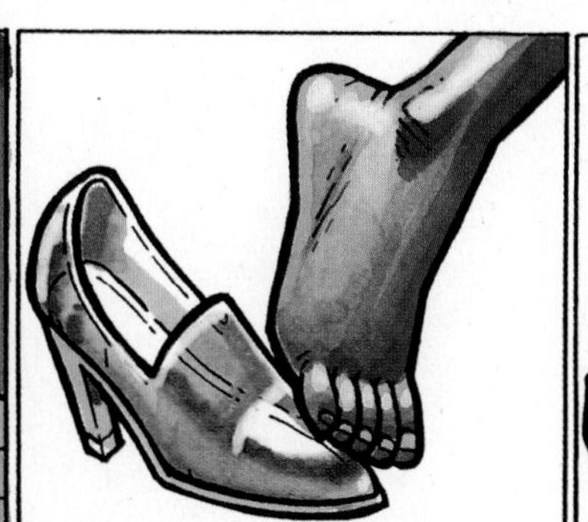

Your views

1 What words have been used to describe Prince Cinders?

2 What sort of person was the fairy?

3 Why did the Princess Lovelypenny like Prince Cinders?

4 If you were one of the big hairy brothers how would you feel about being a house fairy?

5 Give an example of how the author has tried to update the story.

6 Say which version of the story you like best, giving reasons for your preference.

Helpful words

rescued muddled disorganised gallant disgusted entertaining humorous furious

Writing

- To write a humorous version of a traditional tale

The Sorcerer's Apprentice

A sorcerer decides to train a young apprentice and teach him to make spells. At first the apprentice is given all the boring jobs but he longs to be able to do the more complicated magic and impress people.

One day the sorcerer has to go out and leaves the apprentice the job of drawing water from the well. He quickly becomes bored with this activity and decides to consult the spell book to get some help with his chores. He finds just the spell to make the broom do all the work – or is it? Confidently he follows the instructions and he is delighted when the broom starts to fill and carry the buckets of water. Very soon there is enough water for the sorcerer's needs but still the broom carries on working and the apprentice is unable to stop it.

In desperation, the apprentice decides to chop up the broom but this only results in more parts to carry out the spell. Gradually, the room fills with water and, just as the apprentice is being swirled off his feet, the sorcerer returns. Immediately he reverses the spell and all returns to normal.

Then he turns his fury on the unfortunate apprentice who is kicked out of the door as his punishment.

In preparation for writing a humorous version of the Sorcerer's Apprentice:

1 Write the changes you are going to make to the main characters:
   - the sorcerer
   - the apprentice

2 Write a short description of your new setting.

3 Write a brief account of the main changes you are going to make to the story.

4 Think of a new title for your story.

The Sorcerer's Apprentice rewritten

Write the new version of the story in your book.
Remember to check your work.

- Look at the language:
  add more imaginative vocabulary
  make sure your tenses are correct

- Look for punctuation errors:
  capital letters
  full stops
  speech marks
  commas
  paragraphs
  question marks
  exclamation marks

- Look for spelling mistakes

The Phantom Tollbooth

Milo's and Tock the dog's adventures have taken them to Dictionopolis, the city of words, where they visit the local market. Here, instead of fruit and vegetables, words and letters are on sale.

"These are for people who want to make their own words," the man in charge informed him. "You can pick any assortment you like or buy a special box complete with all the letters, punctuation marks, and a book of instructions. Here, taste an A; they're very good."

Milo nibbled carefully at the letter and discovered that it was quite sweet and delicious – just the way you'd expect an A to taste.

"I knew you'd like it," laughed the letter man, popping two Gs and an R into his mouth and letting the juice drip down his chin. "A's are one of our most popular letters. All of them aren't so good," he confided in a low voice. "Take the Z, for instance – very dry and sawdusty. And the X? Why, it tastes like a trunkful of stale air. That's why people hardly ever use them. But most of the others are quite tasty. Try some more."

He gave Milo an I, which was icy and refreshing, and Tock a crispy crunchy C.

"Most people are too lazy to make their own words," he continued, "but it's much more fun."

"Is it difficult? I'm not much good at making words," admitted Milo, spitting the pips from a P.

"Perhaps I can be of some assistance – a-s-s-i-s-t-a-n-c-e," buzzed an unfamiliar voice, and when Milo looked up he saw an enormous bee, at least twice his size, sitting on top of the wagon.

"I am the Spelling Bee," announced the Spelling Bee. "Don't be alarmed – a-l-a-r-m-e-d."

Tock ducked under the wagon, and Milo, who was not over fond of normal-sized bees, began to back away slowly.

"I can spell anything – a-n-y-t-h-i-n-g," he boasted, testing his wings. "Try me, try me!"

"Can you spell good-bye?" suggested Milo as he continued to back away.

The bee gently lifted himself into the air and circled lazily over Milo's head.

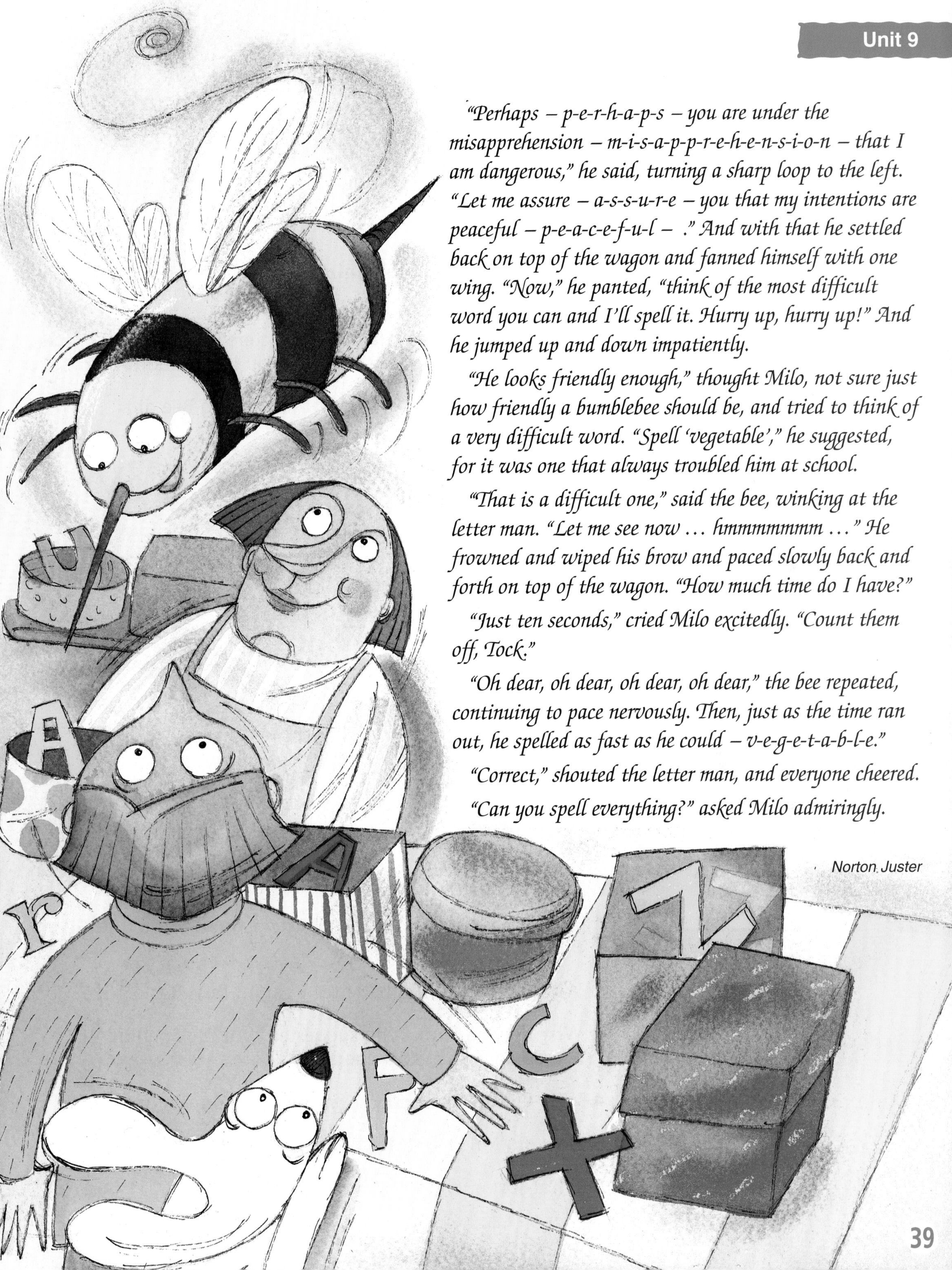

"Perhaps – p-e-r-h-a-p-s – you are under the misapprehension – m-i-s-a-p-p-r-e-h-e-n-s-i-o-n – that I am dangerous," he said, turning a sharp loop to the left. "Let me assure – a-s-s-u-r-e – you that my intentions are peaceful – p-e-a-c-e-f-u-l – ." And with that he settled back on top of the wagon and fanned himself with one wing. "Now," he panted, "think of the most difficult word you can and I'll spell it. Hurry up, hurry up!" And he jumped up and down impatiently.

"He looks friendly enough," thought Milo, not sure just how friendly a bumblebee should be, and tried to think of a very difficult word. "Spell 'vegetable'," he suggested, for it was one that always troubled him at school.

"That is a difficult one," said the bee, winking at the letter man. "Let me see now … hmmmmmmm …" He frowned and wiped his brow and paced slowly back and forth on top of the wagon. "How much time do I have?"

"Just ten seconds," cried Milo excitedly. "Count them off, Tock."

"Oh dear, oh dear, oh dear, oh dear," the bee repeated, continuing to pace nervously. Then, just as the time ran out, he spelled as fast as he could – v-e-g-e-t-a-b-l-e."

"Correct," shouted the letter man, and everyone cheered.

"Can you spell everything?" asked Milo admiringly.

Norton Juster

Comprehension

- To become familiar with the style of an author

The city of words

Use words or phrases to answer these questions:

1 What did these letters taste like?
A Z X I C

2 Write three words beginning with **A** that the Spelling Bee spelt.

3 Make a list of the different characters in this text. Beside each, write one fact that you know about them.

4 Copy which of these actions the Spelling Bee did:

paced slowly back and forth
cleaned himself
jumped up and down
fanned himself
sat on top of the wagon
flew above Milo's head
ate a letter
tested his wings

Market day

1 Why did the letter man say that we don't use **Z** and **X** very often?

2 What do you think the letter **F** might have tasted like?

3 Why do you think Milo suggested that the Spelling Bee should spell the word goodbye?

4 Why did the Spelling Bee wink at the letter man?

5 How did Milo's feelings about the Spelling Bee change?

6 What sort of character is the Spelling Bee?

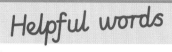

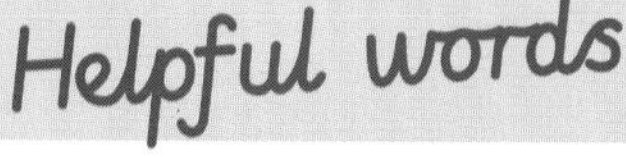

unusual infrequently
pretending frightened
nervous admired
changeable audience

Inventing a character

Writing

- To write an additional episode to a story

You are going to introduce a new character to the story called the Repeating Robin.

First you need to decide what your character is like and how he will behave.

To help you, answer these questions:

1. What adjectives might you use to describe Repeating Robin?
2. What unusual thing does he do?
3. What is his personality like?
4. How does he feel about the other characters?
5. What happens in the marketplace?
6. How is the problem solved?

Tip

Look at the picture for ideas.

Repeating Robin's name could be a clue to the unusual thing that he does.

The Repeating Robin

Write an additional episode to this story.

Use the new character you have invented in your new scene.

Remember:

- make the original characters behave as they always have
- explain exactly what the characters are doing
- make sure you explain how they are feeling
- use description as well as dialogue.

Tip

Your story should be in the style of a funny, imaginary tale.

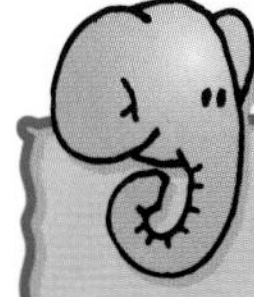

Remember

Dialogue is **conversation** in a story or play.

Hidden Pollution

Pollution kills!

Over the last fifty years, pollution has become one of the most serious problems facing our world. It chokes rivers, smothers life in the oceans, damages the soil and poisons the air.

Pollution is the presence in the environment of large quantities of dangerous chemicals, many created by people, that can harm life and cause long-lasting damage to our planet.

Hidden dangers

If a tanker spills its oil, or we drop litter in the street, we can see it immediately. But some sorts of pollution are more difficult to detect.

Many power stations burn coal that causes acid rain.
In some countries forest fires cause thick smog, blocking out the sunlight. When the trees are gone, they can no longer clean and refresh our air.
Some chemical works send out fumes that damage the atmosphere.
Diesel fumes are thought to cause asthma.

- Smoke and fumes can cause global warming. This is when the upper layers of the Earth's atmosphere act like a greenhouse, increasing the temperatures all over the world.
- The chemicals in some smoke can also mix with the rain and fall on trees hundreds of miles away. This acid rain can cause trees to lose their leaves and even die.
- Fumes from lorry and car exhausts carry invisible particles which we then breathe. It is thought that many people's asthma is caused by these exhaust fumes.

Sadly, it is future generations that will inherit our legacy of failing to care for our environment. What will they be saying about us in 100 years' time?

Adapted from Pollution and Wildlife *by Michael Bright*

Both sides of the argument

Some pollution is difficult to avoid, but we need to be aware of the damage it does to our environment.

Make a table to show how both points of view need to be considered. The first part has been done for you.

Cause of pollution	Benefits we gain	The bad effects of pollution
1 Power stations	Electricity for heating and lighting our homes. Electricity for running TVs, computers, washing machines, fridges, etc.	Chemicals in the smoke make acid rain that can damage trees and crops.
2 Forest fires		

Comprehension

- To recognise two sides to an argument and how the argument has been presented

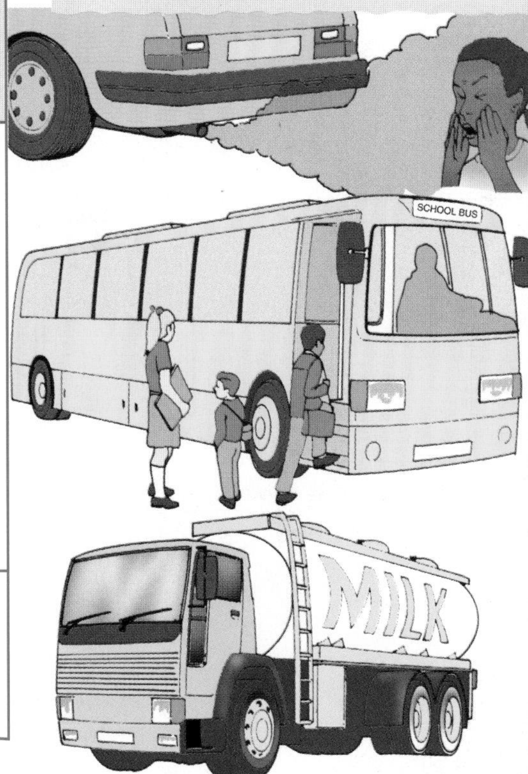

Responding to the issues

1. Why do you think that pollution became so much worse over the last fifty years?
2. Why do you think the writer thinks pollution is one of the most serious issues facing our world?
3. Why does the passage describe fumes as 'hidden dangers'? What other types of pollution can you think of that are not 'hidden'?
4. What do you think the writer might want us to do about the problem of pollution?
5. What is meant by 'future generations that will inherit our legacy'?
6. What do *you* think people will be saying about us in 100 years' time?

Helpful words

emphasis assumes
industries society
improve appreciate
concern action

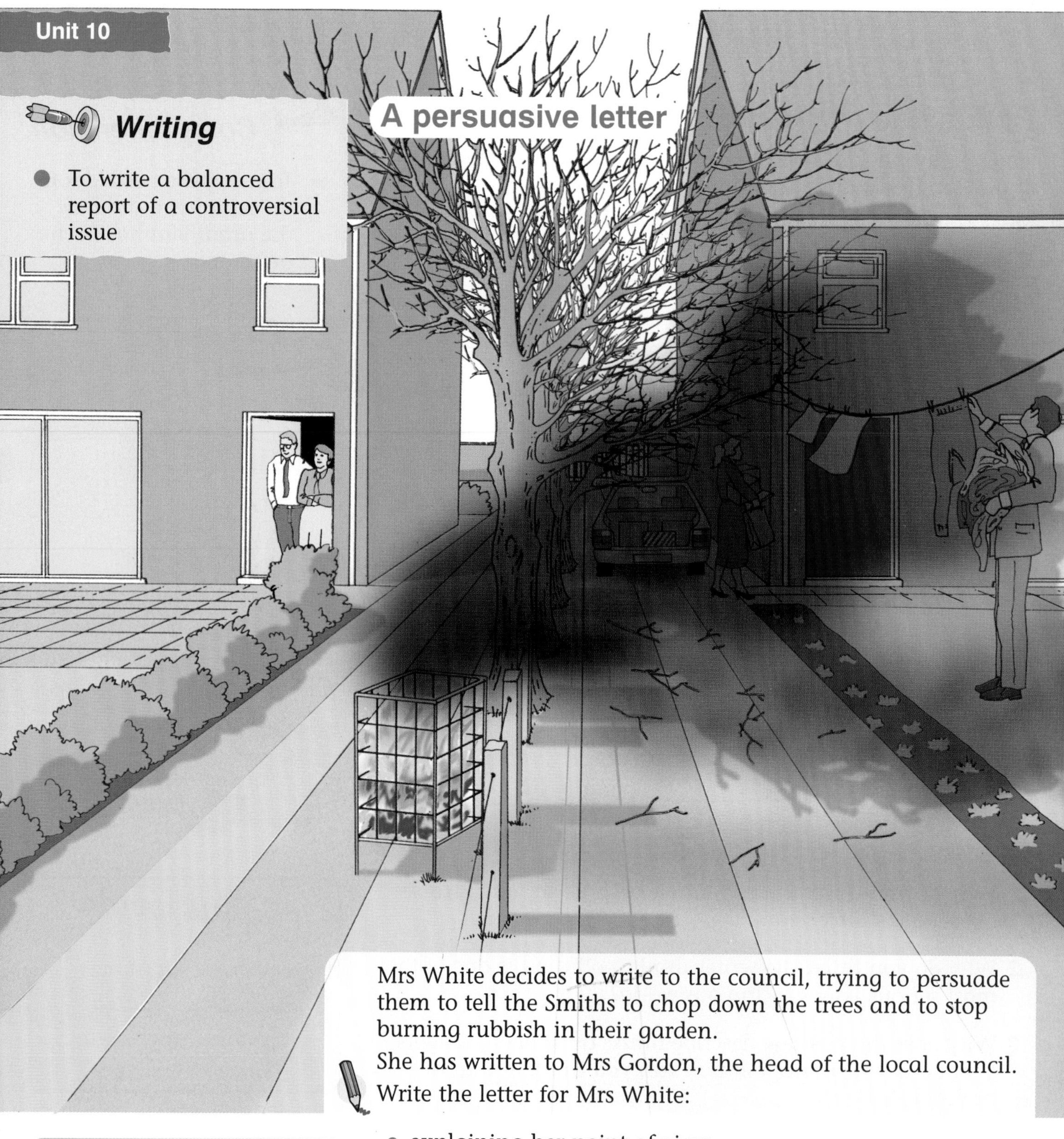

Writing

- To write a balanced report of a controversial issue

A persuasive letter

Mrs White decides to write to the council, trying to persuade them to tell the Smiths to chop down the trees and to stop burning rubbish in their garden.

She has written to Mrs Gordon, the head of the local council.

Write the letter for Mrs White:

- explaining her point of view
- stating what problems occur
- saying how the problems affect their lives
- making proposals for a solution
- asking for Mrs Gordon's support.

Helpful words

blocking interfering
difficulty ruining
impossible compromise

Mr Potter's report

Mr Potter has been asked by the council to visit the homes of the Smiths and Whites. He has to make a report about Mrs White's request to force the Smiths to cut down the trees that form the boundary between them, and to stop the nuisance from the bonfire smoke.

Copy this writing frame to help you to present Mr Potter's findings.

Remember

You should try to report the views of both families as fairly as you can.

The dispute is about __________

Mr and Mrs White say __________

They also say __________

But Mr and Mrs Smith argue that __________

They claim that __________

My opinion is __________

because __________

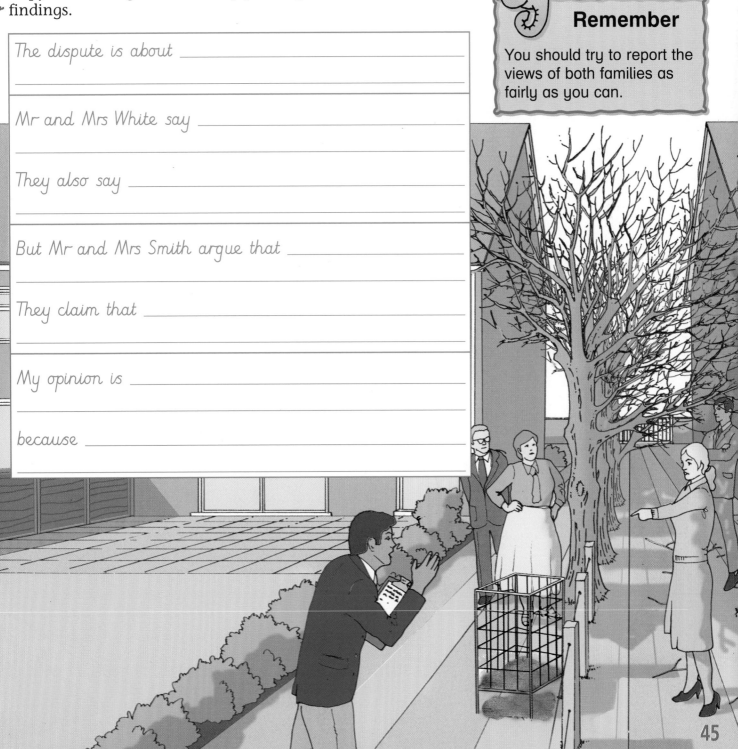

The Midnight Fox

Here are the opening paragraphs of The Midnight Fox.

Sometimes at night when the rain is beating against the windows of my room, I think about that summer on the farm. It has been five years, but when I close my eyes I am once again by the creek watching the black fox come leaping over the green, green grass. She is as light and free as the wind, exactly as she was the first time I saw her.

Or sometimes it is that last terrible night, and I am standing beneath the oak tree with the rain beating against me. The lightning flashes, the world is turned white for a moment, and I see everything as it was – the broken lock, the empty cage, the small tracks disappearing into the rain. Then it seems to me that I can hear as plainly as I heard it that August night, above the rain, beyond the years, the high, clear bark of the midnight fox.

To begin with, I did not want to go to the farm. I was perfectly happy at home. I remember I was sitting at the desk in my room and I had a brand new $1.98 Cessna 180 model. I was just taking off the cellophane when my mom came in. I was feeling good because I had the model, and all evening to work on it, and then my mom told me in an excited way that I was going to Aunt Millie's farm for two whole months. I felt terrible.

Betsy Byars

Setting the scene

Fill in the missing words or phrases:

1 When the boy first saw the fox she was leaping ____________

2 On the last terrible night he was standing beneath the oak with ____________

3 In the flashes of lightning he sees everything as it was – the ____________, the ____________ and the small tracks.

4 He heard the high, clear bark of the midnight fox, ____________ the rain and ____________ the years.

5 He did not want to go to the farm because ____________

Comprehension

- To recognise how an author uses flashbacks

Flashbacks

1 Where is the main character when he is thinking about the summer on the farm?

2 What reminds him of the events of a few years ago?

3 What does the author mean by the fox being 'light and free as the wind'?

4 What do you think is the significance of the empty cage?

5 Why do you think the character especially remembers the 'high, clear bark of the midnight fox'?

6 Why do you think he did not want to visit the farm?

7 What evidence is there to show this story is American?

8 In the passage there are four different locations and times. Write sentences describing each one.

Helpful words

escaped captured
final anxious
bedroom memory
terrible beating
constructing

Writing

- To write a story using flashbacks

Planning a story

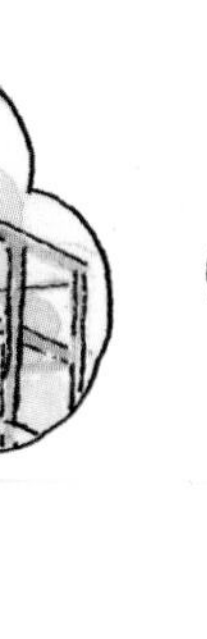

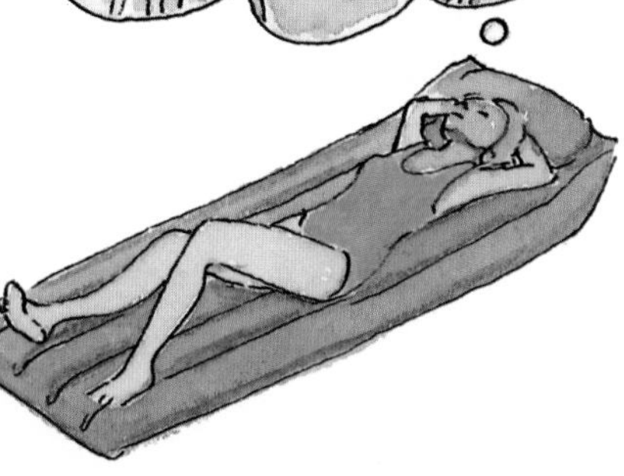

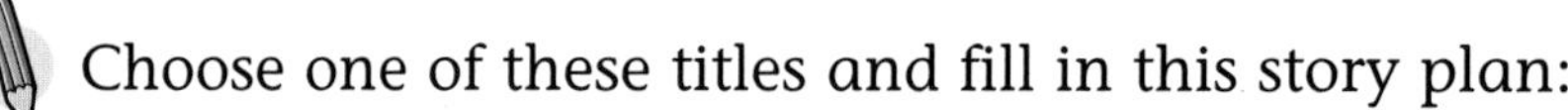

Choose one of these titles and fill in this story plan:

Emergency Call | *The Day I Shrank* | *The Strange Footsteps*

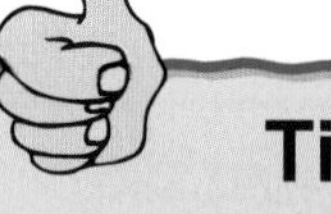

Tip

Do not have too many characters as the plot can become very muddled.

Title	
Characters	
Setting or settings of the main part of the story	
The plot	
How the story ends	

Using flashbacks

1 Start your story by having your main character in a different setting reflecting back over the main event of your story.
Here is an example:

George looked out of the window as the train passed through the outskirts of a town. He thought how all towns look the same from a train. Suddenly he caught sight of a small boy kicking a football. In a flash, his mind jumped back two years, to another child, just like the one with the football. He would never forget the panic on the face of the child on that dark November evening. The boy had shouted for help, but no one was near enough to hear – except George.

Tip

Your story should have this pattern:

- a situation that triggers the memory
- the memory of the climax of the story
- a flashback to the start of the day when the event took place
- how the story was resolved.

2 Then start your account of the story earlier in the day.

It had been a cold, foggy night when George had decided to call for his friend Zac. Zac's mother brushed aside all his protests and insisted homework should be done before he could go out to play. George wandered away down the road, kicking a stone, wondering what he would do.

3 Now finish writing your story.

Joining the Library

These children have decided to join their library. They have had the leaflet and they thought it would be good to join – there are not only thousands of great books to look at, but computers with the Internet, CDs, help with homework and lots of other things there, too.

So just what library help can I get?
• Free books, hundreds of them!
• Free membership for life, starting from the day you're born
• Helpful, trained staff able to make reading fun and stress free
• Help with homework - reference collections, access to information on computers, and maybe homework clubs
• School holiday activities
• Any book from anywhere - you can order books specially
• Newspapers & magazines
• Computers - in lots of libraries you can now use computers and get on the Internet
• Storytimes - check out if your library has storytimes, they're brilliant for making friends and getting children started on words
• Parents' information collections
• What's on - you can get information about what's on in your area
• Different things to borrow - you may be able to borrow storytapes, CDs, videos, even computer games. And some libraries have childminder tickets that let you borrow even more books
LaunchPad
Promoting the value of libraries for children
Everybody's hair

So that he can understand the sorts of things people want from the library, the man behind the desk has asked them to fill in a questionnaire.

Name ______________________________

Address ______________________________

Tel No. ____________

Age ________ D. of B. ________

Name of parent/guardian ______________

Please tick or cross

Have you visited a library before? Yes ☐ No ☐

Have you been a member of a library before? Yes ☐ No ☐

Which of the following activities are you likely to be interested in?

borrowing books ☐ using the computers ☐
holiday clubs ☐ homework clubs ☐
author readings ☐ borrowing CDs ☐

Which types of books are you most interested in?

- fiction books ☐
  adventure ☐ fantasy ☐
  romance ☐ sci-fi ☐
  traditional tales ☐ myths and legends ☐
- poetry books ☐
- non-fiction books ☐
  sports ☐ birds ☐ animals ☐
  hobbies ☐ fashion ☐ dancing ☐
  other countries ☐ transport ☐ music ☐
- other (please state) ______________________

How often are you likely to visit the library?
(Please tick)

monthly ☐ every two weeks ☐
once a week ☐ more than once a week ☐

Comprehension

- To understand how questionnaires and pamphlets obtain and provide information

Matching answers

Match the question with the correct answer. It is important to read all the questions and answers before you begin.

1 Why do the children think it might be good to join the library?	Reference books, information on computers and homework clubs can all make homework easier.
2 Why have they been asked to fill in a questionnaire?	Story tapes, CDs, videos and computer games can all be borrowed from the library.
3 What is the information in the leaflet encouraging children to do?	The questionnaire helps the staff to understand what services people most want from their library.
4 How can a library help with their homework?	They like the ideas they have seen in the leaflet.
5 What other things can be borrowed from a library besides books?	The leaflet encourages the children to use the wide variety of services available.

Helpful words

beginning support
promotes time-consuming
extend respond
enable provides
enjoyable

Passing on information

1 Write the four most important services that you think a library provides.

2 Why do you think the project has been given the title Launch Pad?

3 Questionnaires often ask people to use a cross or a tick. Why do you think this is?

4 What changes might the librarians make as a result of this questionnaire?

5 Are libraries important? Give reasons for your opinions.

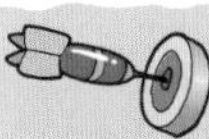

Writing

- To create an effective questionnaire

Creating effective questions

When collecting information in a questionnaire you need the answers to give you all the detailed information you want. The questions therefore need to be carefully worked out.

Remember

Wherever possible provide a selection of responses which only require a tick.

A group of children have been asked to research whether the school should start an after-school club. They have drafted the questions below for their questionnaire. Rewrite them so that more useful information is collected.

1 Would you like an after-school club on Wednesdays?

2 Does your mum or dad go out to work?

3 Do you like sport?

4 Would you like it to last for one hour?

5 Would you like help with maths homework?

6 Do you walk home after school?

Organising a questionnaire

To make an effective questionnaire you need to group the questions carefully. Use the information below to create your questionnaire about the after-school club.

Remember your questions must provide useful information for the club organisers.	When you create your questionnaire use these categories for your questions.
• Which age groups of children, and how many, might come to a club. • When the club should meet. • What activities they need to provide that aren't already provided by other clubs. • Whether they need to arrange to help children get home later.	• About the person, including where they go after school. • About whether they would come to the club, and how many times a week. • About how often and for how long the club should meet. • About other things the person does after school. • About what they would like to do in the club. • About the type of help they might like with homework. • About how they could get home afterwards.

Kidnapped

Alan and David are fleeing for their lives from the redcoat soldiers. They have reached a river but fear they can go no further and may be cornered.

So there we stood, side by side upon a small rock slippery with spray, a far broader leap in front of us, and the river dinning upon all sides. When I saw where I was, there came on me a deadly sickness of fear, and I put my hand over my eyes. Alan took me and shook me; I saw he was speaking, but the roaring of the falls and the trouble of my mind prevented me from hearing; only I saw his face was red with anger, and that he stamped upon the rock. The same look showed me the water raging by, and the mist hanging in the air; and with that, I covered my eyes again and shuddered.

The next minute Alan had set the brandy bottle to my lips, and forced me to drink about a gill, which sent the blood into my head again. Then, putting his hands to his mouth and his mouth to my ear, he shouted, "Hang or drown!" and turning his back upon me, leaped over the farther branch of the stream, and landed safe.

I was now alone upon the rock, which gave me the more room; the brandy was singing in my ears; I had this good example fresh before me, and just wit enough to see that if I did not leap at once, I should never leap at all. I bent low on my knees and flung myself forth, with that kind of anger of despair that has sometimes stood me in stead of courage. Sure enough, it was but my hands that reached the full length; these slipped, caught again, slipped again; and I was sliddering back into the lynn, when Alan seized me, first by the hair, then by the collar, and with a great strain dragged me into safety.

Never a word he said, but set off running again for his life, and I must stagger to my feet and run after him. I had been weary before, but now I was sick and bruised, and partly drunken, with the brandy; I kept stumbling as I ran, I had a stitch that came near to overmaster me; and when at last Alan paused under a great rock that stood there among a number of others, it was none too soon for David Balfour.

Robert Louis Stevenson

On the run

Copy and fill in the gaps with one or more words.

A ______________ was an obstacle to David and Alan escaping the redcoats. David was very ______________ and Alan tried to ______________ him to jump over the ______________ water. Alan set a ______________ to his lips and forced him to ______________; he then turned and ______________ over the stream. David knew that if he did not ______________ he would not have enough ______________ to do it. With a surge of anger, he threw himself at the opposite bank, and was only prevented from falling back into the ______________ by Alan's strong grip that ______________ him to safety. Alan then set off running again and David, bruised and ______________, stumbled after him. They ran until they came to a great ______________, where they ______________ to catch their breath.

Comprehension

- To identify features of a text that build suspense

Helpful words

hearing sickness
shuddered chance
escape roaring
desperate exhausted
determined created
atmosphere panic
raging feelings

Keeping their nerve

1 Write two phrases that tell us David was very frightened.

2 How do we know the water was flowing very quickly?

3 Write what you think Alan was trying to say to David.

4 Find these words in the passage, and from the way they are used, work out their meanings:

dinning (paragraph 1)
gill (paragraph 2)
stead (paragraph 3)
overmaster (paragraph 4)

5 Here are five things David *did*. Write how he *felt* about each of them. The first one has been done for you. Use a different phrase for each one.

Standing at the edge of the river – *very frightened*
Standing alone on the rock before the jump –
As he jumped –
Running after Alan –
Resting under the rock –

6 Do you think the author has created suspense in the passage? How do you think he has achieved it?

Writing

- To write a passage creating suspense

Feeling afraid

At some time in your life you will have felt afraid. (It is nature's way of helping you to cope with danger, real or imagined.)

Write a short passage about what happened and how you felt.

Use your senses:

- Sight – details of what you saw around you
- Sound – any unusual noises or conversations that you heard
- Smell, touch, taste – these might come into your account depending on your situation
- Feelings – how you reacted to events; what it made you do.

Fleeing from danger

Write part of a story where your characters are running away from something that frightens them.

Before you start decide:

- who your characters are and a little about what they are like
- the setting they are in and how it changes
- how they both feel during the chase
- what happens to stop the suspense and make the reader feel relieved about the outcome.

Use at least three paragraphs in your writing.

Paragraph 1 – Set the scene and start the action.

Paragraph 2 – Build up the tension of the action and describe how your characters are feeling.

Paragraph 3 – The situation is resolved.

Tip

If you use two characters you can make it clear how they feel and how they react to each other.

An Equal Chance

Just as a bigger child can bully a smaller one in school, so a bigger group of people can treat a smaller group unfairly simply because they have a different religion, language or way of life. That dislike is called **prejudice**. Treating people unfairly because they are different is called **discrimination**.

People are often discriminated against because they are slightly different from the others in a group:

- they have a different colour skin
- they have a different religion
- they are old
- they are young
- they are taller, shorter, fatter or thinner
- they are disabled or handicapped in some way.

We will all dislike someone at sometime. That is natural. It only becomes prejudice when we dislike people because of things they either cannot change or should not be asked to change. The colour of their skin, their shape or size or looks, the way they worship God or the way people of their culture live their lives should not alter how someone is treated or stop them having equal rights with everyone else.

What has all this to do with me?

It is not only governments or powerful leaders who persecute people. Individuals, too, can take away the rights of others. It happens in little ways, in school, in shops, or in our street.

We all show prejudice every time we let our dislike or fear of an individual or a group lead us to say or do things which are unfair. It is when we act on our dislikes that such prejudice becomes dangerous – when we will not let people who are different join our group in the playground; when we insult them or bully them or allow them to be insulted or bullied without making a fuss.

People who bully and discriminate are often frightened and scared. They usually get together in gangs because they are cowards – not brave enough to speak or act alone. But the dilemma we all have to face is when and how to stand up for someone who is being discriminated against. That needs courage, real courage, especially if the bullies are usually our friends.

Adapted from Equal Rights *by Maureen O'Connor*

Comprehension

- To understand the different attitudes or views on a controversial issue

What does it mean?

Write a definition for the following words. Think about the context where each word appears in the passage. Use a dictionary to help you.

bully

prejudice

discrimination

rights

dilemma

Where do you stand?

1 What can you do to stop prejudice and discrimination?

2 Why do you think that some people are prejudiced?

3 Give an example of how a coward might behave.

4 What aspects of people's lives should they not be asked to change, and why?

5 What do you think the author means by 'making a fuss'?

6 Make a list of some reasons why people might be discriminated against.

Helpful words

responsibility consider
support ignorant
unthinking frightened
pretend fundamental
belief informing
friendship

Writing

- To write guidance for others that is clear and meaningful

Advice for someone who is being bullied

Bullying often occurs in schools, but if we understand how to deal with it, the problem can usually be resolved. It is useful to have some suggestions for children being bullied, but remember that they will need several options as situations can vary enormously.

Here are a few suggestions made by children when they talked about bullying in their class:

Ask the bully how they would feel.
Don't fight back as it might make matters worse.

Try to talk the bully out of what he or she is doing.
Go and play somewhere else.
RUN! YELL! TELL!

Make a list of other suggestions that you think might help someone being bullied.

Try to present the suggestions as a wallchart in a fun way so that the reader feels better.

Jokes and sayings decorating the edges might be a good idea.

Remember:

- The person may need a cooling-off time before following some of the ideas.
- Handling the situation yourself, if possible, is often the best point to start from.
- If the matter is serious you may need to involve others.
- You are trying to make the person feel better about themselves so they will have the confidence to deal with it.

Tip

Make sure you have written in clear sentences so that the information can be quickly understood.

Helping the bully

1 Make a list of all the reasons why you think someone bullies someone else.

2 How might you persuade a bully to behave differently?

Remember:

- You need to get them to think about what they are doing.
- Try to encourage them to use their energy in a different way.
- Explain how they can put things right when they have made a mistake.
- Say how much better they will feel if they get their problem sorted out.

Tip

Bullies:

- want attention
- are being bullied themselves
- think it's cool to bully.

The Wind

Praise Song of the Wind

Trees with weak roots
I will strike, I the wind.
I will roar, I will whistle.

Haycocks built today
I will scatter, I the wind.
I will roar, I will whistle.

Badly made haycocks
I will carry off, I the wind.
I will roar, I will whistle.

Uncovered stacks of sheaves
I will soak through, I the wind.
I will roar, I will whistle.

Houses not tightly roofed
I will destroy, I the wind.
I will roar, I will whistle.

Hay piled in sheds
I will tear apart, I the wind.
I will roar, I will whistle.

Fire kindled in the road
I will set flickering, I the wind.
I will roar, I will whistle.

Houses with bad smoke-holes
I will shake, I the wind.
I will roar, I will whistle.

The farmer who does not think
I will make to think, I the wind.
I will roar, I will whistle.

The worthless slug-a-bed
I will wake, I the wind.
I will roar, I will whistle.

Traditional Siberian poem translated by W Radloff and Willard R Trask

The Wind

The wind is a wolf
That sniffs at doors
And rattles windows
With his paws.

Hidden in the night,
He rushes round
The locked-up house
Making angry sounds.

He leaps on the roof
And tries to drive
Away the house
And everything inside.

Tired next morning,
The wind's still there
Snatching pieces of paper
And ruffling your hair.

He quietens down and in the end
You hardly notice him go
Whispering down the road
To find another place to blow.

Stanley Cook

The Wind

I can get through a doorway without any key,
And strip the leaves from the great oak tree.

I can drive storm-clouds and shake tall towers,
Or steal through a garden and not wake the flowers.

Seas I can move and ships I can sink;
I can carry a house-top or the scent of a pink.

When I am angry I can rave and riot;
And when I am spent, I lie quiet as quiet.

James Reeves

Comprehension

- To compare the way different poets have written about the same subject

Two poems

The Wind by Stanley Cook

1 With what does the wind rattle the windows?

2 How does the wind feel when it is 'ruffling your hair'?

3 Why don't you notice the wind the next day?

The Wind by James Reeves

4 What does the wind do to the oak tree?

5 How can the wind 'get through a doorway without any key'?

6 What does the poet mean by the phrase 'when I am spent'?

7 Which of the three poems do you like best ? Why?

Helpful words

quietens underneath
energy imagination
draughts whispering

Similarities and differences

Sort these statements so that they are written under the correct poem heading in the table below.
You may need to write some of them in more than one column.

When the wind is quiet it is described as sleeping.	The poem ends with the wind being very gentle.
Lines that are repeated in each verse.	The poem uses sounds to describe the wind.
The poem is written in the first person.	The last word rhymes in each pair of lines.
The wind blows on the roof.	The end of the second and the fourth lines rhyme.
The ends of the lines do not rhyme.	The setting is the countryside.
It seems as if the wind is boasting about what it can do.	The moods of the wind change through the poem.

The Wind by Stanley Cook	Praise Song of the Wind	The Wind by James Reeves

Writing

- To annotate and evaluate a poem

Annotate a poem

Copy out the poem *Praise Song of the Wind* in the centre of a piece of plain paper so that there is room to write comments around it.

Underline the text that is referred to and annotate your ideas at the side.

An example is given to help you.

Trees with weak roots
I will strike, I the wind,
I will roar, I will whistle.

Haycocks built today
I will scatter, I the wind,
I will roar, I will whistle.

Badly made haycocks
I will carry off, I the wind,
I will roar, I will whistle.

conical heaps of hay in a field

Uncovered stacks of sheaves
I will soak through, I the wind,
I will roar, I will whistle.

Houses not tightly roofed
I will destroy, I the wind,
I will roar, I will whistle.

Hay piled in sheds
I will tear apart, I the wind,
I will roar, I will whistle.

Fire kindled in the road
I will set flickering, I the wind,
I will roar, I will whistle.

Houses with bad smoke-holes
I will shake, I the wind,
I will roar, I will whistle.

The farmer who does not think
I will make to think, I the wind,
I will roar, I will whistle.

The worthless slug-a-bed
I will wake, I the wind
I will roar, I will whistle.

1 What are:
haycocks?
stacks of sheaves?
smoke-holes?

2 What is meant by:
houses not tightly roofed?
worthless slug-a-bed?

3 Find and annotate the part of the poem that indicates the wind will bring rain.

4 Underline in red all the verbs that tell you what the wind will do.

5 Indicate the verse that you like best and say why.

6 How will the wind make the farmer think?

Tip

To annotate your work, write at the side and draw a straight line to the part you are referring to.

Writing to the editor

You want this poem to be included in the next issue of a magazine.

Write a short letter to the editor to give your reasons why you think this poem should be included.

Remember to say:

- what you like about it
- why it would be suitable for the magazine
- in which month you think it should be included
- who you think would enjoy reading it.

A Question of Marriage

This is a story from Somalia in Africa.

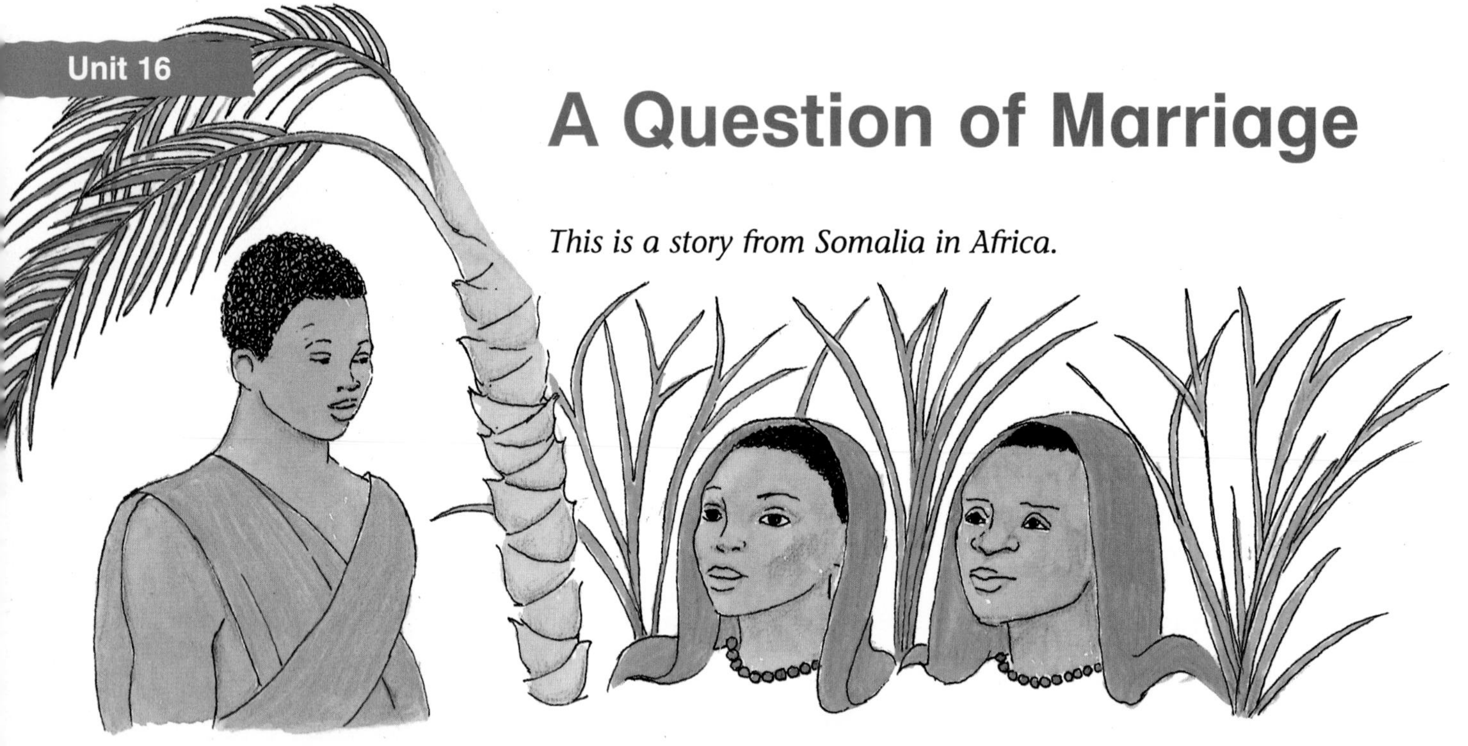

Once there were two sisters. One was beautiful and stupid. The other was plain but clever. One day a young man came to their village looking for a wife. At first he couldn't take his eyes off the beautiful sister. Then he talked to the plain one. She didn't dazzle him like her sibling but she talked a lot of sense.

The man was confused. "What should I go for," he wondered, "beauty or intelligence?"

He decided to go and see Kabacalaf, the wise man of the village. Kabacalaf said, "Ask both sisters three questions. The one who gives you the right answers shall be your bride."

The young man listened to Kabacalaf's questions. Then he went to see the beautiful sister.

"What is the best blanket a man can sleep on?" he asked.

"One made of fibre and grass," said the beautiful sister promptly.

"And what is a camel's pen?"

"That's rather a silly question," giggled the beautiful sister. "It's a high fence that keeps the camels in at night."

"I see," said the young man. "And now can you tell me what is the best sauce to eat with boiled millet?"

"Of course I can," said the beautiful sister without thinking. "The best sauce to serve with millet is melted ghee and milk."

"Thank you," said the young man. He went along to see the plain sister.

"Tell me," he said, "what is the best blanket a man can sleep on?"

"Peace of mind," said the plain girl, "for without peace of mind no one can sleep a wink."

"What is a camel's pen?" asked the young man.

"A camel's pen is man himself, for it is man who herds the camels together for safety at night."

"And what is the best sauce to serve with boiled millet?" came the last question.

The plain sister thought for a while. Then she said, "The best sauce to serve with millet is hunger because when you are hungry everything tastes delicious."

The young man was most impressed with her answers. She had spoken most wisely.

Now he knew what his decision would be. He realised the plain sister would make a caring, wonderful companion who would share his problems and give him advice. So he asked her to marry him – and she agreed.

Retold by Saviour Pirotta

True, false or can't tell

Copy these sentences.

Write *true*, *false* or *can't tell* next to each one.

1 *The young man was confused because he didn't know which sister to marry.*

2 *The beautiful sister wore fine clothes and jewellery.*

3 *The second question he asked was what sauce should be served with boiled millet.*

4 *The plain sister said that a high fence kept the camels in at night.*

5 *The plain sister said that peace of mind would help him to sleep.*

6 *The plain sister said she would make the young man hungry.*

7 *The plain sister won the hand of the young man because she had answered wisely.*

8 *The young man thought that the plain sister would be a good cook and keep his house clean.*

Stupid or clever?

1 What clues are there in the text that tells us this story comes from Africa?

2 What was different about the way the sisters answered the young man's questions?

3 Why was it important for the young man to choose carefully?

4 Find the word in the text that has a similar meaning to:
impress sister quickly partner

5 Explain what the phrase 'peace of mind' means.

6 What do you think the storyteller wants us to learn from this story?

Comprehension

- To answer literal questions

Helpful words

character thoughtful
considered future
prosperity important
customs advice

Writing

- To write an extended story based on a proverb

Only start what you can finish

> *The eye makes the heart desire,*
> *The heart makes the eye look.*

In *A Question of Marriage* when the heart made the eye look, the man discovered that the plainer sister would make the better wife.

Here is a plan for the first two chapters of an extended story called *Only Start What You Can Finish.*

Chapter One

Setting	Characters	Plot
A busy residential street. Bay-windowed terraced houses with small patches of garden in the front.	● Joe, an eleven-year-old boy, enthusiastic and keen to help others, can be over-ambitious. Medium height, brown hair, dressed in scruffy school uniform. ● Polly, his sister, cheerful but inclined to want her own way. Dark curly hair, neat school uniform. ● Mr Jones, elderly neighbour, frail, white hair.	Two children arguing on their way home from school. They notice Mr Jones working in his garden and then collapsing. He explains that he's getting ready for a visit from his son who is just returning from the navy. Polly takes him inside and makes a cup of tea. Joe promises to finish sorting out his garden and starts working on it but is unable to finish it and promises he'll complete it the next day.
Later: At home in the kitchen. Mum is busy making tea, the children are helping. Everything is rather chaotic.	Mum busy and harassed, kindly and caring. Can be quick-tempered.	Conversation in the kitchen. Mum says she has tickets for the new film they've all been wanting to see. They are for the next day. Polly says that Joe can't go as he's promised to finish the garden. Joe has a problem.
Later that evening: By the phone.	Peter, James and Mark, friends from school.	Conversation on the phone organising his friends to help very early next morning.

Chapter Two

Setting	Characters	Plot
Joe and friends approach Mr Jones's garden. Early morning deliveries are being made.	Nick, the scrap metal dealer. Wearing old battered hat driving a very old open-back truck.	Conversation, friends grumbling about the early start. Joe notices the truck and has an idea. Conversation with Nick who lets him have an old anchor and chain and other bits from the truck. Boys work hard to finish and Mr Jones is surprised and delighted when he looks out.
Later: The garden is changed. The hedge is cut into the shape of a ship, the chain and anchor border the path, shells decorate the front of the flower bed.		Boys walk away pleased with what they've done. Mr Jones suggests they might do other gardens, perhaps with a different theme – maybe Star Wars!

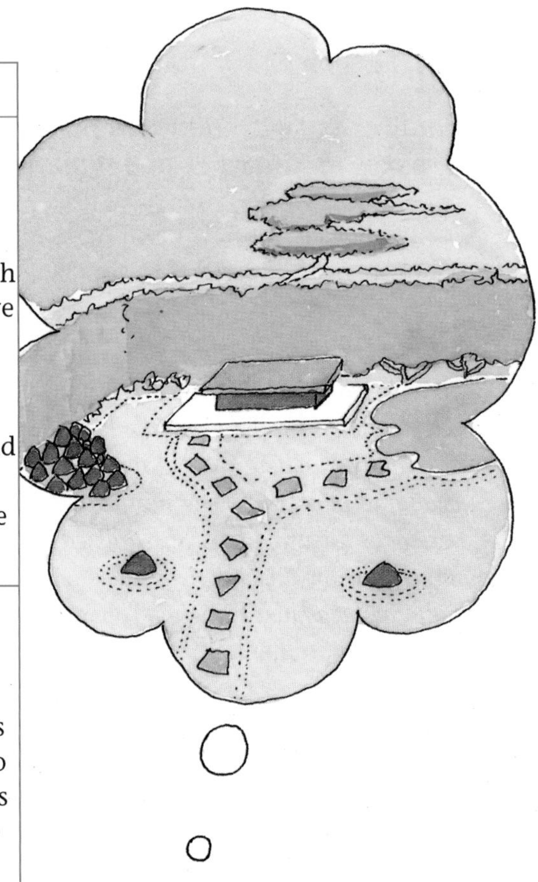

Use the plan to write the first chapter of your extended story.

Use the plan to write the second chapter of your story.

A space garden

Write another chapter for this story.

The idea of a Star Wars garden might help you.

Maybe the boys have been asked to tidy up the area around some swings and climbing frames. What do they use to make the garden this time and who is it for?

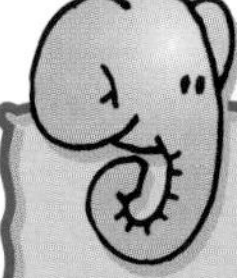

Remember

Use speech marks carefully when writing dialogue (conversations) in your story.

A New Home

Heidi

Heidi lives in Switzerland and has gone to live with her grandfather. She wakes up after her first night in her new home.

Heidi was awakened next morning by a shrill whistle and as she opened her eyes a beam of sunlight came through the hole in the wall, making the hay shine like gold.

At first she could not think where she was, then she heard her grandfather's deep voice outside and remembered joyfully that she had come to live in the mountains. She had been glad to leave old Ursula, who was very deaf and felt the cold so much that she sat all day by the kitchen fire or the living-room stove. Heidi had had to stay indoors where the old woman could see her, though she often longed to run outside and play. Now she jumped out of bed, full of excitement at all the new experiences awaiting her. She dressed herself as quickly as possible, then climbed down the ladder and hurried outside. Peter was waiting there with his herd and her grandfather was just bringing Topsy and Dusky from their stall. She went to say good morning to them all.

Johanna Spyri

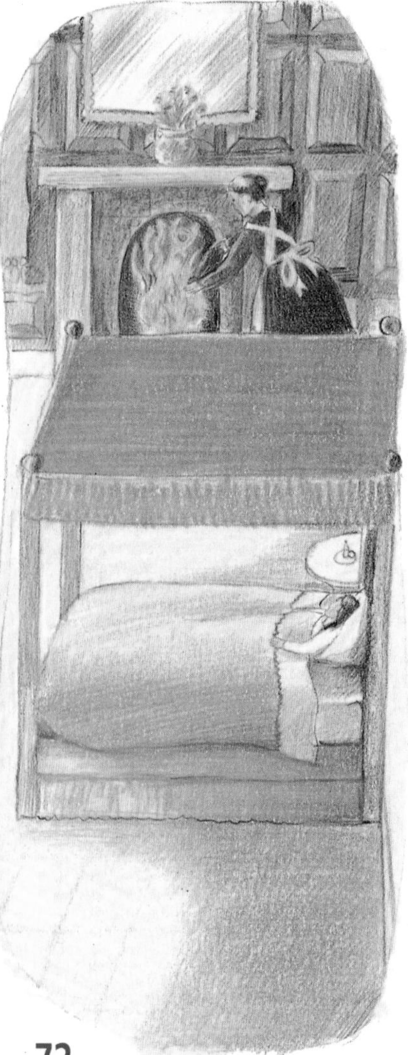

The Secret Garden

Mary has travelled from her home in India to be taken care of by her uncle who lives in England. She wakes up after her first night in her new home.

When she opened her eyes in the morning it was because a young housemaid had come into her room to light the fire and was kneeling on the hearth-rug raking out the cinders noisily. Mary lay and watched her for a few moments and then began to look about the room. She had never seen a room at all like it, and thought it curious and gloomy. The walls were covered with tapestry with a forest scene embroidered on it. There were fantastically dressed people under the trees, and in the distance there was a glimpse of the turrets of a castle. There were hunters and horses and dogs and ladies. Mary felt as if she were in the forest with them. Out of a deep window she could see a great climbing stretch of land which seemed to have no trees on it, and to look rather like an endless, dull, purplish sea.

"What is that?" she said, pointing out of the window.

Martha, the young housemaid, who had just risen to her feet, looked, and pointed also.

"That there?" she said.

"Yes."

"That's th' moor," with a good-natured grin. "Does tha' like it?"

"No," answered Mary. "I hate it."

"That's because tha'rt not used to it," Martha said, going back to her hearth. "Tha' thinks it's too big an' bare now. But tha' will like it."

Frances Hodgson Burnett

Waking up

Use words and phrases to complete these sentences:

1 *Heidi was woken by the sound of a ________, while Mary was woken by the sound of ________*

2 *When Heidi awoke she felt ________ but Mary looked around the room and thought it looked ________*

3 *Heidi had gone to live in the ________ while Mary had gone to stay on the ________*

4 *Before she got out of bed Mary ________ while Heidi remembered ________*

5 *When she got out of bed, Heidi felt ________ because ________*

6 *Mary lay in bed and questioned ________ about ________*

7 *Heidi was pleased with the new day so she went outside to say ________*

8 *We know Mary was not happy because she told the housemaid ________ the moor.*

Comprehension

- To compare similar situations in stories by different authors

Tip

Reread the sentences to make sure you have included all the words you need.

Helpful words

familiar apprehensive
uncomfortable flashbacks
descriptions curious
excited joyful
strange

Contrasts

1 Why do you think the two girls reacted differently to waking up in a new place?

2 What evidence is there in both passages that these stories were possibly written a long time ago?

3 What different ways have been used to set the scene in each passage?

4 What do we know about Heidi's character from the text?

5 What do we know about Mary's character from the text?

6 Briefly say what you think might happen to Heidi in this book.

7 Using the clues in the text say what you think might happen to Mary.

8 Which passage do you prefer? Why?

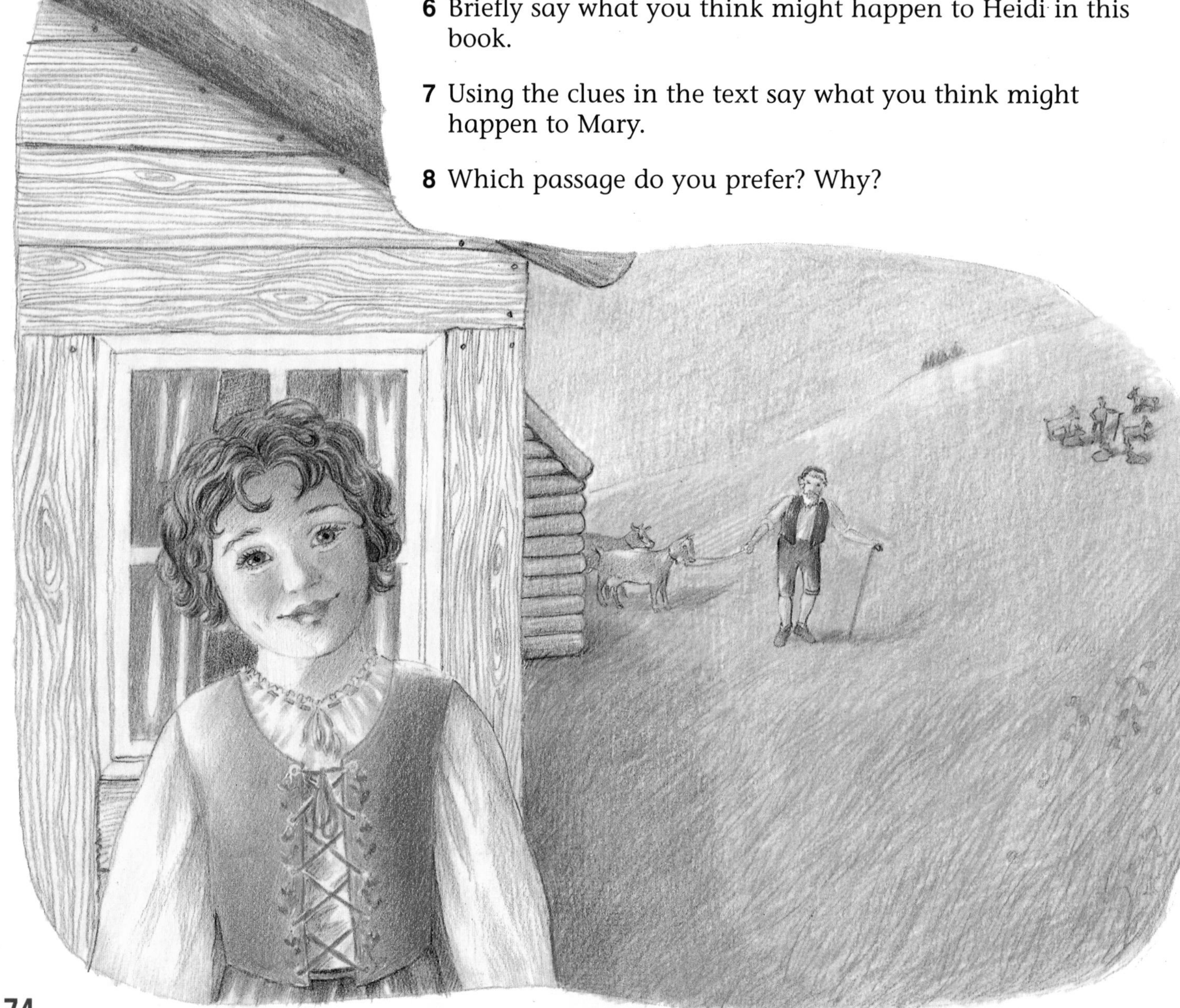

Writing a comparison

Use the comprehension you have been working on to write a comparison between the two passages.

Write the title:

A Comparison of Two Texts: Heidi and The Secret Garden

In your writing:

- note the similarities and differences of the two main characters
- explain how the different characters react to the new situation
- say how the reader is made to feel about the characters
- state what parts you liked best and why.

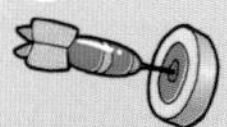

Writing

- To write a comparison of the two texts

Helpful words

For example they both
they are also similar
where the characters differ
both texts develop
a contrast in the settings
uses dialect
uses dialogue
uses a flashback
my opinion is
After looking at the different texts
Finally I would like to say

Heidi and Mary

Imagine that the characters Heidi and Mary have met in the setting in the picture.

Write the story of what happens when they try to rescue the stranded child.

Make up your own title for your story.

Tip

Think what you know about their characters before you write about what they would do and say.

Dangers in a Victorian Factory

Early factory work was unhealthy and dangerous, as were many other Victorian jobs. The only concern of most factory owners was making money. They did not worry about the health and safety of their workers. There were always many people willing to work in the factories, even if the conditions were poor. Until laws were made to protect the workers, the owners were not forced to think about safety.

A child cleaning a working machine

Safety at work

Can you see the child under the machinery in the picture on the left? Children had to clean fluff away from the machinery while it was still running. This could be very dangerous. Imagine what would happen if workers caught their hair or clothes in the machinery while they were working or leaning over it.

In 1884 a law was passed to force cotton mill owners to put guards over the moving parts of some of their machinery, but it was not until much later that all factories had to protect their workers in this way.

Punishment

Children were often so tired from working long hours that they could not work quickly or concentrate. Men in charge of the children kept them at work by shouting at them or punishing them. Look at what is happening in the picture on the right. A beating like this was quite a common event in some factories. A few overseers were very cruel. For example, a common punishment in one nail-making factory in the Midlands was to drive a nail through the worker's ear into the wooden bench. There were no laws to protect children against such cruelty.

A factory overseer beating a child worker

Glossary

overseer *supervisor*

Chemical danger

Workers often had to use dangerous chemicals in their work. For example, phosphorus was used to make matches. Its fumes could damage a matchworker's bones. Phosphorus made teeth drop out and even jaws rot away. Until the later part of the Victorian period, there were no laws to punish employers for unhealthy working conditions.

Working conditions

Factories could be very crowded and very noisy. There were no rules about how many people could work in one factory, or whether there was too much noise from the factory machinery.

In a Victorian factory, workers would spend hours in a noisy, crowded room with poor lighting. The atmosphere could be stuffy in summer or cold with no heating in winter. Just imagine what the noise would be like for the women in this photograph with all those tightly-packed machines working in the same room.

Women workers in a cotton mill in Lancashire

Industrial illnesses

If people became ill at work, their family or friends took them home. There were no doctors or nurses working, even in the largest factories. Workers were given no money as compensation by the factory owners if their illness or injury was caused by bad working conditions. In fact, workers who missed a day's work, missed a day's pay. Workers who could no longer work ended up in the workhouse, unless their family could support them and look after them. It was only after 1895 that some workers were given compensation for industrial illness.

Adapted from A Victorian Factory *by Lyn Gash and Sheila Watson*

Comprehension

- To scan text quickly to locate information

Tip

Scan the text to find key words to help you.

Scanning for answers

Note the time that you start this section and then work as quickly and efficiently as you can.

You do not need to write a full sentence for these answers.

1 Why was it dangerous for the children to work under the machinery?

2 What were the factories like in the summer?

3 What chemical was used to make matches?

4 What effect did phosphorus have on the factory workers?

5 If you were too ill to work, where might you live?

6 Why were the children so tired?

7 What law was passed in 1884?

8 After what year was compensation paid to the workers?

9 Why did factory owners not worry about the health and safety of some of their workers?

10 How did the men in charge keep children working?

More than the text

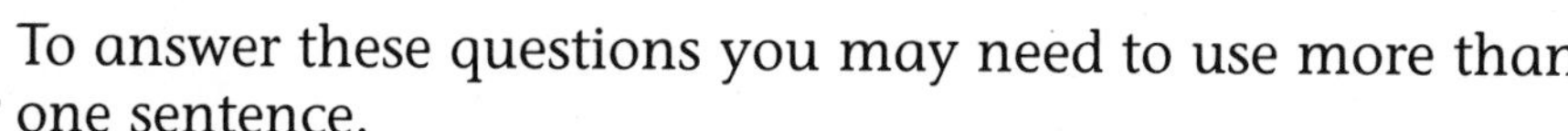

To answer these questions you may need to use more than one sentence.

1 What was the attitude of most factory owners to their workers? Explain why they felt this way?

2 How do you think the overseer decided which jobs the children and adults should do?

3 Do you think that the punishments that were used on the children would make them work harder? What else might the factory owner have done?

4 How do you think the conditions in the factories affected the workers? What effect did this have on the factory owners?

5 Why do you think new laws were brought in to improve the conditions for the workers?

Helpful words

competition production
employment strength
energetic comfortable
healthy inefficient
exhausted understand
cooperation efficiency

Organising information

Imagine that you are a young person living in Victorian times. You and your friends are very scared of your factory owner, but you believe something must be done about your working conditions.

You decide secretly to produce a leaflet to send to MPs, and others who never see inside a factory, to try to get the conditions improved for all factory workers.

Make brief notes or lists about what you are going to include on each side.

Here are some suggestions:

Side one – slogan and picture, to attract attention

Side two – a list, using bullet points, of the most important issues you want to highlight

Side three – brief description of a typical day for a child factory worker

Side four – what you would like to see done, and what effect this would have

Side five – 'before' and 'after' pictures to add impact to the changes you want

Side six – a general message asking everyone to support your ideas.

Writing

- To create a leaflet that is well organised and clear to other people

Making your leaflet

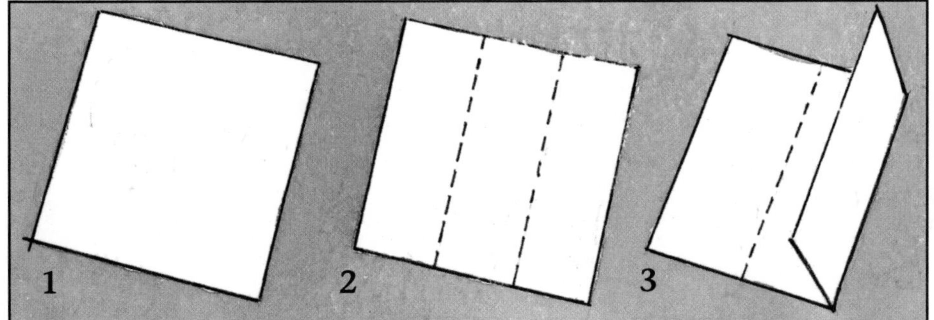

Use the diagrams to help you fold your piece of paper to make your leaflet. It should have six sides to it. Lightly number them in pencil.

When you write your leaflet you will need to check:

- the spelling of difficult words
- whether you need to cut down the information to fit
- whether what you have said is clearly expressed
- whether you have fulfilled the purpose of the task.

Tip

Use bullet points, different colours and size of print, headings, sub-headings and illustrations to help make your leaflet more interesting.

Book Covers

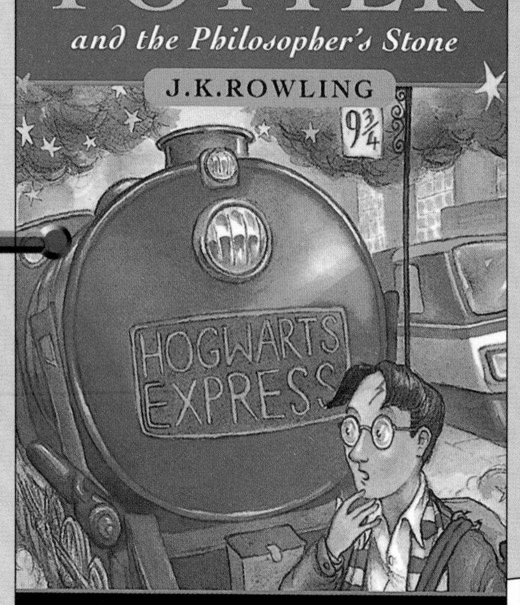

HARRY
POTTER
and the Philosopher's Stone
J.K.ROWLING
9¾
HOGWARTS
EXPRESS
Winner of the 1997 Smarties Gold Award

We are first attracted to books by the look of the front cover but quickly we turn them over to find out more.

Harry Potter thinks he is an ordinary boy – until he is rescued by an owl, taken to Hogwarts School of Witchcraft and Wizardry, learns to play Quidditch and does battle in a deadly duel. The Reason: HARRY POTTER IS A WIZARD!

Acclaim for Harry Potter and the Philosopher's Stone:

"This is a story full of surprises and jokes; comparisons with Dahl are, this time, justified." *The Sunday Times*

"... Harry Potter and the Philosopher's Stone has all the makings of a classic... Rowling uses classic narrative devices with flair and originality and delivers a complex and demanding plot in the form of a hugely entertaining thriller. She is a first-rate writer for children." *The Scotsman*

"A richly textured first novel given lift-off by an inventive wit." *The Guardian*

"A terrific read and a stunning first novel." *Wendy Cooling*

BLOOMSBURY
£4.99
ISBN 0-7475-3274-5
9 780747 532743
http://www.bloomsbury.com

Extracts from newspaper book reviews praising the book and skill of the author.

HOW TO LOOK AFTER YOUR PET

FISH

How to choose your new fish

•

Preparing cold-water and warm-water tanks

•

What to feed your fish, and when

•

How to keep your fish happy and healthy

Fish is one of an exciting new series of pet care books designed to help young animal owners look after their pets. Illustrated on every page with full-colour photography, **Fish** is packed with practical information on every aspect of fish care.

Mark Evans is a qualified vet who writes widely about pet care. He often appears on television, most recently as presenter of the popular BBC TV children's series, *Wild Bunch*

Other titles in the series
Kitten · Puppy · Guinea Pigs
Rabbit · Hamster · Birds

ISBN 0-7513-5400-7
9 780751 354003
DK
A DORLING KINDERSLEY BOOK
www.dk.com
£4.99

HOW TO LOOK AFTER YOUR PET FISH

DORLING KIND

A DORL

HOW

A PR

The kind of information you can find.

About the author.

About other books in the same series.

WINNER OF THE SMARTIES BOOK PRIZE
WINNER OF THE CHILDREN'S BOOK AWARD

Tells us it has been recommended for awards.

HIGHLY COMMENDED FOR THE CARNEGIE MEDAL

No-one can ever be like a mother to us.
NO-ONE. NO-ONE AT ALL.
ESPECIALLY NOT STUPID FRIZZY DIZZY ROSE.

Ruby and Garnet are ten-year-old twins. Identical. They do *everything* together, especially since their mother died three years earlier. But can being a double act work for ever? When so much around them is changing...

'Another winner by Jacqueline Wilson... impossible to put down'
THE SCHOOL LIBRARIAN

'An exuberant story... irresistible' GUARDIAN

'Written with enormous vitality and wit... the story never falters'
JUNIOR EDUCATION

SHORTLISTED FOR THE YOUNG TELEGRAPH/FULLY BOOKED AWARD
SHORTLISTED FOR THE NOTTINGHAMSHIRE CHILDREN'S BOOK AWARD

Illustrated by Nick Sharratt (Ruby)
and Sue Heap (Garnet)

Introduces the main characters.

Quotes from book reviews.

Tells us it has been recommended for awards.

KINDER

LOOK AFTER YOUR PET
FISH
GUIDE TO CARING FOR YO
MARK EVANS

This is an extract from the book.

'The door of the room began to open. Chas could have screamed. The door had no right to open. It no longer existed . . .'

Death stalks a gang of leather-clad bikers. A ghostly female voice lures a man into danger. And Chas wakes up to terror when he finds a First World War soldier in his bedroom . . . twenty years after he was supposed to have died . . .

Here in eight short stories from a master thriller writer are mystery, excitement, the baffling tricks of time – *and the overwhelming power of the supernatural . . .*

Cover illustration by Barry Jones

UK £3.99

ROBERT WESTALL *The Haunting of Chas McGill*

ROBERT WESTALL
THE HAUNTING OF CHAS McGILL
AND OTHER STORIES

This is written to encourage the reader to buy or read the book.

Comprehension

- To understand the usefulness of book blurbs

Which book?

Match the statements to the correct book:

Statements	Books
What to feed your fish.	Harry Potter and the Philosopher's Stone
Strange happenings and ghostly characters appear.	How to Look after Your Pet Fish
A first novel.	Double Act
A book about twins.	The Haunting of Chas McGill and Other Stories
This book has won prizes.	
The author appears on television.	
Witchcraft and wizardry feature in this book.	
Illustrated using photographs.	
Written by a master thriller writer.	

Helpful words

imagination amusing eye-catching shadow emphasis information expectations factual italic photography artwork bold humorous mysterious sequel

Extended answers

These questions require longer answers as you need to give details about your opinions.

1 What do you notice about the print that has been used on the book covers? Why do you think there is a variety?

2 Make a list of the things from a book cover that encourage you to read the book. What do you think is most important and why?

3 How are fiction and non-fiction book covers different? Why do you think this is?

4 Look at how colour and illustrations have been used. What do you like or dislike about them?

5 Which book do you think you would most like to read? Give reasons for your choice.

Back covers for storybooks

Writing

- To write a story summary for the back cover of a book

Go back to pages 32–33 and reread the story of Prince Cinders.
Now write what you would put on the back of the book.
These points will help you:

- include a short piece of the text
- write a short introduction to the characters and the story
- quote from a book review praising the book
- quote from a book review praising the skill of the author
- list two or three other titles written by the author.

Use a plain piece of paper to design the layout for the back cover.

Tip

Think about the kind of lettering you want to use.

Back covers for information books

Look at the back cover of the book about fish.
Now write and design the back cover for a book, in the same series, about cats.
These points will help you:

- use a similar title
- write a few sentences about the information you could find in the book, and how it is presented
- comment on the quality of the illustrations and photographs
- give some information about the author
- list two or three other titles in the series.

Use a plain piece of paper to design the layout for the back cover.

Tip

If you vary the size of the print, important points can be emphasised.

Fitness Exercises

Whatever your favourite sport, fitness training is a vital part of a player's everyday routine. Below you will find important exercises to use before you start to exercise vigorously. It is very important to warm up properly if you are to avoid damaging your muscles.

Warming up

- While standing, slowly rotate your head clockwise and anticlockwise. Now move it from side to side, and up and down.
- Stand straight, and raise both your shoulders together, then push down. Now lift one shoulder up and down, then the other.
- With your arms by your sides, shake your hands for a few seconds. Now swing your arms back and forth, then rotate them in large circles.
- With your arms by your sides, stand upright with your feet together. Slowly bring one knee up to your chest and then the other.
- With your feet slightly apart, bend down and touch your left ankle with your right hand. Now use your left hand to touch your other ankle.
- Stand with your feet together and arms at your side. Jump with your arms and legs outstretched, then bring them back again.

Stretching

Groin stretch

Bend down on one knee, stretching your other leg out behind you. Slowly push yourself down towards the floor and hold for ten seconds. Now stand up, change legs and repeat.

Side bends

Stand with your feet slightly apart. Bend over to one side as far as possible, bringing the opposite arm over your head. Hold and count to ten, then change sides.

Touching your toes

From a standing position, slowly reach down and touch your toes, keeping your legs straight. Now stand up again.

Ankle clasps

Keeping your legs straight, bend down and clasp one ankle with both hands. Slowly push your head down towards your hands and hold for ten seconds. Repeat using the other ankle.

From Improve Your Soccer Skills *by Paula Woods*

Selecting statements

Write only the statements that apply to this text.

It uses headings and sub-headings.

An introduction to explain the purpose of the table has been used.

Very few adjectives have been used.

The author tries to build up tension.

The activities have been numbered.

Bullet points have been used for emphasis.

The sequence of each activity is easily understood.

A glossary has been used.

It has been written in the present tense.

Comprehension

- To identify features of a non-fiction text

Preparing to play

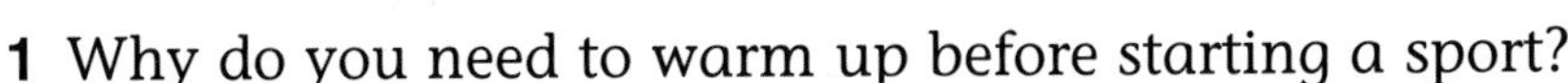

1 Why do you need to warm up before starting a sport?

2 Why should these activities be done every day?

3 Why should you only rotate your head slowly when you are warming up?

4 Do you think these activities should be numbered? Give reasons for your opinion.

5 What parts of the body do you think you are stretching when you do ankle clasps?

6 Stretching builds up suppleness. What kind of activities would you suggest for strength and stamina (the ability to undertake activity for a long time)?

Helpful words

damage strain
fitness healthy
muscles maintain
ordered quickly
prolonged effort

Writing

- To set out clearly a non-chronological text

Tip

You may need to add your own headings and change some words.

Tackling – making a good job of it

To make a good footballer you need to know how to tackle.

The following information will give you some ideas, but it has been written as one continuous block of text.

It is your job to rewrite this to make it clearer.

Paragraphs, bullet points, order numbers or headings could be useful.

The purpose of tackling is to try to deprive your opponent of possession and gain it for yourself. When the opponent has the ball you should quickly close down the space between you, slow down as you get close, so that you are balanced, challenge the opponent by tackling and then quickly clear the ball by passing to another team member or dribbling away at speed. There are two kinds of tackles: a block tackle and a sliding tackle. In a block tackle you need to approach the attacker from one side, keep your eyes on the ball and strike the ball just as the attacker is about to pass the ball. If the ball becomes stuck between you, try flicking it over their feet. In a sliding tackle you are aiming to clear the ball. Timing is very important as you could injure your opponent and give away a free kick. The tackle should come across the front of the opponent and push the ball away from their feet. Afterwards you need to get to your feet as quickly as possible to continue playing your part in the game.

Spotlight sport

Choose a sport that you know about and write an information page about it.

Try to include a variety of ways of presenting your ideas so that the reader remains interested and learns more about your sport.

Tip

Plan your work carefully so that you are not attempting to do too much.

Weather

January new beginning,
Resolutions,
Snowflakes spinning.

February frosty fogs,
Winter shivers,
Fire-warm logs.

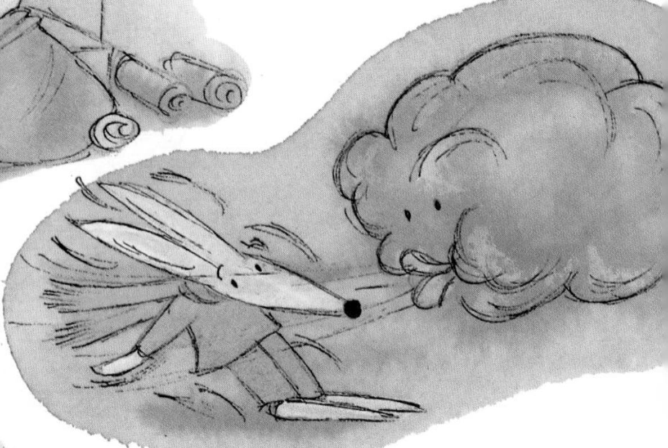

March blows windy, smells of spring,
Leaves peek out,
Brave blackbirds sing.

April showers fall soft and slow,
Earth wakes up,
And green things grow.

May Day ribbons round a pole,
May-time babies
Lamb and foal.

June brings summer blazing in,
Scent of roses,
Sun on skin.

July joy means schools are out,
Time for picnics,
Heat and drought.

Lucy Coats

Months of the year

Write the correct answer in your book:

1 In what month are we likely to see snow?

January February March

2 What happens in March?

Winter shivers blackbirds sing Earth wakes up

3 When do the green things grow?

when there are smells of spring
when brave blackbirds sing
when the Earth wakes up

4 What 'brings summer blazing in'?

May June July

5 In which month might you be short of water?

February June July

6 What might you be doing when lambs and foals are being born?

having a picnic
shivering by a fire
dancing round a pole

Comprehension

- To recognise how a theme is developed in a poem

Patterns and changes

1 Which month does not mention the weather?

2 What does it mean in the first verse when it says 'resolutions'?

3 What does the phrase 'Earth wakes up' mean?

4 Why are most young animals born in the spring?

5 Why are we now very careful about 'Sun on skin'?

6 Make a list of the words that mention the different kinds of weather we have.

7 What patterns are there in this poem? Think about rhyme, the number of lines in a verse and how you think the poem would continue.

Helpful words

promises strength
plenty improve
hibernation cancer
protection

Writing

- To write a sequence of verses for a poem

Collecting ideas

Collect words or phrases for the remaining months of the year that:

- describe the weather
- describe something that happens in nature in that month
- describe something that most people do in that month
- explain how you feel in that month.

Here are some ideas for August. You can add some more of your own if you wish.

August

scorching sun, cloudless sky, long sunny days, hot, dusty city streets, poppies bloom in fields, warm seas, peas popping from their pods, holidays by the sea, dripping ice creams, barbecues, lazy, relaxed, put your feet up time, thick, heavy diesel fumes, dried brown grass in the parks

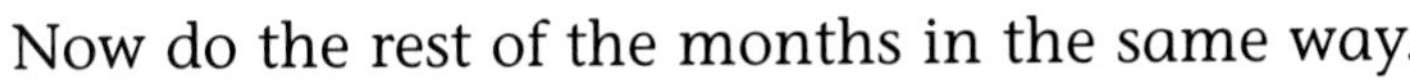

Now do the rest of the months in the same way.

September

October

November

December

Completing the cycle

Use the ideas you have written to help you compose verses for the rest of the months of the year.

You will have more material than you need, so select very carefully.

- Your **first** line should start with the name of the month and make a statement about it. This can be a longer line.
- Your **second** line should be short and have no more than three words.
- Your **third** line should also be short.

When you have written a verse check that the rhythm fits with the earlier verses by reading them together.

When you have finished, write your poem neatly in your book.

Remember

You need to do this on scrap paper so that you can edit your work to improve it.

Tip

The rhythm is the **beat** of the lines in the poem.

Netiquette

> Login.

> OK everybody, sit up straight! It's about time we taught you some manners. Just like RL, the Net has its own rules about being polite. The code is known as netiquette. If you go round offending people, you're just asking to be **flamed**!

> DON'T SHOUT!

> Shouting (using capital letters in messages) is considered bad manners. Only shout when you have something really important to say. Shouting in **newsgroups** is especially frowned upon because it is difficult to read.

> Keep your sig short!

> A long signature is considered most inappropriate. Remember, the longer the signature, the longer the person at the other end has to wait while it downloads!

> Never correct people's spelling mistakes!

> This will turn you into instant flamebait. People typing quickly make lots of little errors. Just ignore them. They may even be deliberate!

> Answer your e-mail immediately!

> Because e-mail arrives so quickly, people get jumpy if they don't receive an instant reply. Calm their nerves by **replying** to your mail as soon as you can. If you're too busy to write a proper letter, just send a one-line message to let them know their mail arrived safely.

> Read the FAQ!

> You'll find a Frequently Asked Questions (FAQ) file in all newsgroups and on some web sites too. Read it! Nothing gets on people's nerves more than having to explain the same things to newbies again, and again, and again...

> Think before you post!

> Before you post a message on newsgroups, remember that 30 million people might read it. Silly or rude remarks will not make you popular!

> HAND!

NETSPEAK

> The Net has its own language and if you want to surf in style, you've got to learn the lingo.

> As well as TLAs and emoticons there are loads of new technical words. Be warned: spelling is notoriously bad on the Net. Sometimes this is due to typing errors but often it is deliberate. For example, numbers may be used for letters such as «3» for «e»; or «8» for «ate», as in L8R (later).

> Here's a guide to some essential Net words and what they mean:

Bounced mail E-mail that comes back because the wrong address was used.

Browser A program for navigating the World Wide Web.

Cyberspace The virtual world of the Internet.

Domain name A name of an address on the Internet.

e-mail The system that allows you to send messages to other people on the Net.

e-zine Like a magazine – only on the Internet!

FAQ Frequently Asked Questions – a list of the most common questions and their answers.

Finger A program that gives you information about someone else who is online.

Flame A crushing put-down or nasty remark.

Flamebait Someone who deserves to be flamed!

Keypals Just like penpals – only you write to them using e-mail!

Login Connecting to your service provider and going online.

Logoff Disconnecting from your service provider.

Lurkers Net users who read other people's messages in newsgroups but do not post any of their own.

Newbie Someone who is new to the Net.

Newsgroup A discussion group on Usenet.

Nick Your nickname on the Internet.

Poster Someone who leaves messages in a newsgroup.

Service provider Also known as an Access provider, a company that sells access to the Internet.

Signature Your personal way of signing off at the end of postings and e-mail.

Snail mail Letters delivered by the postman.

Spam To send someone junk e-mail, or leave useless postings in a newsgroup.

World Wide Web A network of files with both text and graphics on the Net that can be accessed using a browser.

From Kids Rule the Internet: The Ultimate Guide *by Jason Page*

Comprehension

- To learn more about the language of computer and electronic communications

Choose the correct answer

1 Why should you keep your signature short?

Short signatures mean that you can be recognised quickly.

You are not allowed to have a long signature.

2 Why should you answer e-mail quickly?

Answering quickly means that the person knows you have received their message.

Until you have answered the e-mails you cannot get any more.

3 When should you use capital letters in messages?

Use capital letters when you want to make something clear.

When you have something important to say you should use capital letters.

4 What is bounced mail?

Letters that pass on from person to person are called bounced mail.

Bounced mail are letters that are incorrectly addressed.

5 What is a keypal?

A keypal is a way of signing off from the Internet.

Someone you have never met that you send e-mails to on the Internet.

6 What do they call a person who reads other people's messages?

A person who reads other people's messages is called a finger.

A person who reads other people's messages is called a lurker.

Understanding the lingo

1 Why must you be careful when you post a message on newsgroups?

2 What are letters delivered by the postman called? Why?

3 How do you think someone would feel if they were sent spam?

4 What must you do to avoid being a flamebait?

5 What are FAQs and why would newbies have to be careful?

An e-mail message

You have just received this e-mail from a friend. Write what his message says, in normal English:

> **When did U call? I w8d till l8. Call yourself a gr8 m8! R U coming 2 football 2night? I'll B there – U B there 2!!**
>
> **C U l8r**
>
> **Harry**

Writing for the Net

1 Compose a message for a friend but include your own quick ways of writing.

Here are some that you might like to use:

2 for too, two or to	*4 for for*
B for be	*C for see*
I for eye	*R for are*
U for you	*Y for why*

2 Now compose your friend's reply using the same method.

Helpful words

annoyed upset
excited exasperated
observe offence
netiquette frequently
irritation

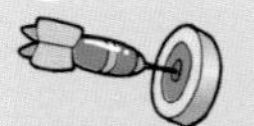

Writing

- To use language adapted for the computer

Tip

The quick methods that you use must be obvious to others or they will not be able to read your message.

PEARSON EDUCATION LIMITED
Edinburgh Gate, Harlow, Essex, CM20 2JE, England
and Associated companies throughout the World.

First published 2000
Third impression 2002

Printed in China GCC/03
ISBN 0 582 40834 2

Acknowledgements
We are grateful to the following for permission to reproduce photographs:
Ardea London page 5 (Jean-Paul Ferrero); Bubbles pages 50 bottom (Ian West) and 59 (Jennie Woodcock); Mary Evans pages 8, 9 left, 76 bottom right and 77; Hulton Getty pages 9 right and 76 top left; Sally and Richard Greenhill pages 50 top, 58 and 84; Pictor International pages 14 left, 24 and 25; Stone page 14 right.

We are grateful to the following for permission to reproduce book covers:
Bloomsbury for *Harry Potter and the Philosopher's Stone*; Corgi Yearling for *Double Act*; Dorling Kindersley for *How to Look After Your Pet Fish*; Macmillan for *The Haunting of Chas McGill.*

We are grateful to the following for permission to reproduce copyright material:
The Arts Council of England and the Department of Culture, Media and Sport for the extract from LaunchPad; Bloomsbury Publishing plc for adapted extracts from *Kids Rule the Internet* by Jason Page; Franklin Watts Inc for extracts from *Equal Rights* by Maureen O'Connor; HarperCollins Publishers for extracts from 'The flea and the sheep' and 'The fig tree' by Leonardo da Vinci from *Fables of Leonardo da Vinci* translated by Bruno Nardini; Independent Newspapers (UK) Ltd for an adapted extract from the article 'Britain's sharks face extinction' by Marke Rowe in *The Independent on Sunday* (11.7.99); The Society of Authors as the literary representative of the Estate of John Masefield for an extract from the poem 'Sea Fever' by John Masefield; Penguin Books Ltd for the text of *Prince Cinders* by Babette Cole (Hamish Hamilton, 1987) Copyright © Babette Cole, 1987; Laura Cecil Literary Agency on behalf of the James Reeves Estate for the poems 'The Sea' and 'The Wind' from *The Complete Poems for Children* by James Reeves published by Heinemann; The Watts Publishing Group Ltd for the poem 'Weather' by Lucy Coats from *First Rhymes* published by Orchard Books 1994.

We have been unable to trace the copyright holder of the poem 'The Wind' by Stanley Cook and would appreciate any information which would enable us to do so.

The handwriting characters in this book were created using *Handwriting for Windows 2.0.* This product enables the user to create model handwriting in the size, colour and style of their choice (including a dotted script). HfW2 runs on Windows 95 and above and is available from KBER (Kath Balcombe Educational Resources). Please contact Customer Services for details on 01743 356764.

Cover Bruce Coleman (Werner Layer)

The publisher's policy is to use paper manufactured from sustainable forests.